First oral contraceptive pill produced in U.S.

King George VI dies at Sandringham.

Parliamentary library is destroyed by fire.

CBC television initiates broadcasting in Toronto and Montreal.

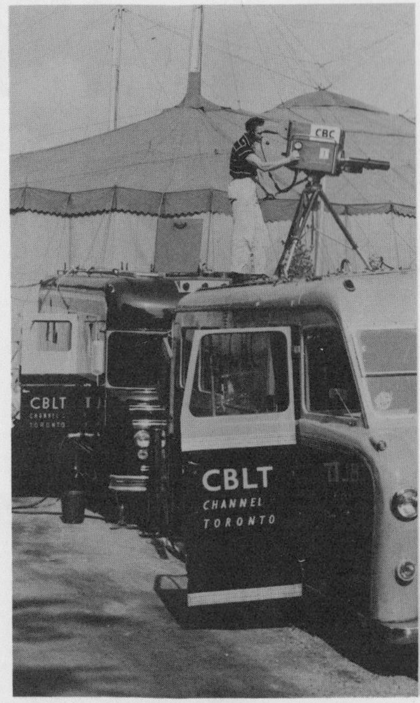

First performance of National Ballet Company.

1953

Alexander W. Matheson becomes premier of P.E.I.

Zinc, lead, copper, silver and pyrite discovered near Bathurst, N.B.

The Trans-Mountain Pipe Line Co. builds oil pipeline from Edmonton to Vancouver.

Coronation of Queen Elizabeth II.

John Diefenbaker is elected to Commons for Prince Albert, Saskatchewan.

Louis St. Laurent leads liberal party to majority victory.

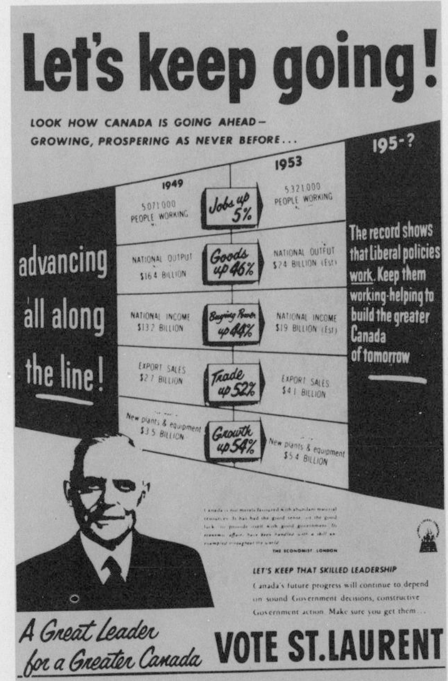

Violence erupts with Doukhobor protests in B.C.

Shakespearian Festival opens in Stratford, Ontario.

Riots erupt at Kingston Penitentiary.

Tornado causes $5 million in damages around Sarnia, Ontario.

Norman Berrill wins Governor General's Award for non-fiction with *Sex and the Nature of Things.*

London Conference of Commonwealth prime ministers.

1954

First iron ore exported from Ungava Range in Labrador.

Hurricane Hazel hits Ontario, Quebec and Atlantic Provinces.

Doug Hepburn wins world weight-lifting championship at Stockholm.

Jean Drapeau elected mayor of Montreal.

Soviet defector Igor Gouzenko wins Governor General's Award for *The Fall of a Titan.*

Dr. Jonas Salk of U.S. develops antipolio vaccine.

British Commonwealth Games held in Vancouver's new Empire Stadium.

Henry D. Hicks becomes premier of N.S.

Dr. Wilder Penfield publishes *Epilepsy and the Functional Anatomy of the Human Brain.*

Marilyn Bell swims Lake Ontario.

The Booming Fifties

July 18, 1959. Canada and the U.S. commemorated the opening of the St. Lawrence Seaway with this first-day cover for stamp collectors.

Alexander Ross

The Booming Fifties 1950/1960

Canada's Illustrated Heritage

Canada's Illustrated Heritage

Publisher: Jack McClelland
Editorial Consultant: Pierre Berton
Historical Consultant: J. Michael Bliss
Editor in Chief: Toivo Kiil
Associate Editors: Clare McKeon
Jean Stinson
Designer: David Shaw
Cover Artist: Alan Daniel
Picture Research: William Bilecki
Lembi Buchanan
Judy Forman
Betty Gibson
Patricia McLoughlin

ISBN: 0-9196-4427-9

NSL, Natural Science of Canada Limited
254 Bartley Drive
Toronto, Ontario M4A 1G4

Printed and bound in Canada

Although the booming fifties witnessed radical changes in Canadian values, the ties of God and country were still strong. The ad above was one in a series on the "Tradition Counts" theme done by O'Keefe Breweries.

Contents

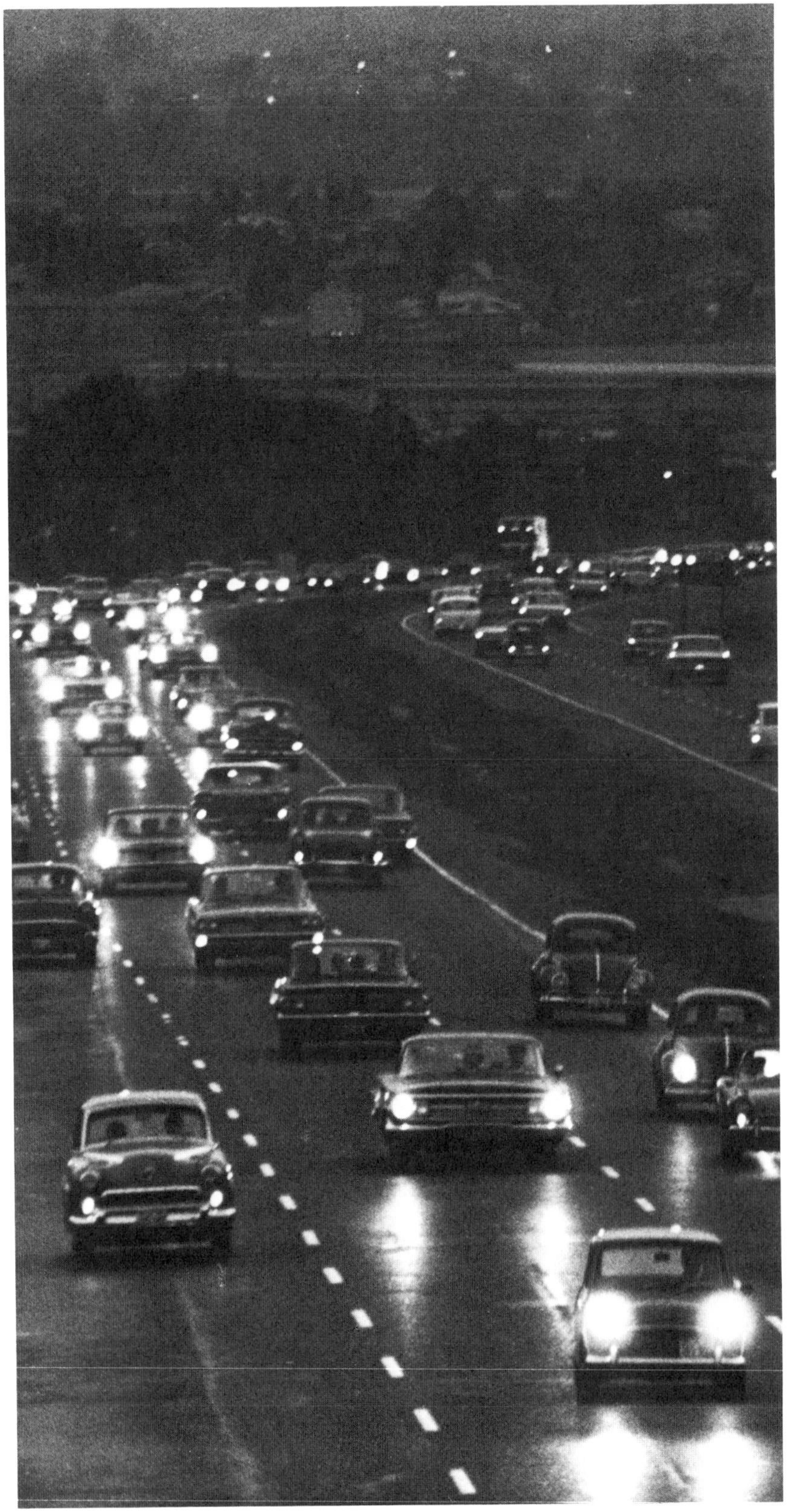

Learning to Live with Bigness

The raw statistics of [1950s] growth in Canada are formidable. . .

William Kilbourn in *The Canadians*

The 1950s: the very name of the decade has become synonymous with a quality of sexual and political innocence that later generations both long for and deride. It was a decade of tranquility and prosperity for Canada, but it was also a time of swift and decisive changes, changes which were largely unheralded as historic, but which transformed our daily lives.

It was in the 1950s that we stopped being shoppers and became consumers. It was the 1950s that shaped the modern Canadian city with its superhighways, suburbs and shopping plazas. It was the 1950s that witnessed Canada's transformation from a loyal outpost of WASPdom to a cultural mosaic that is republican in all but name. It was in the 1950s that we first discovered youth. We began the decade by worrying about teenagers and ended it by emulating them. We also discovered the most potent cultural force of all, television, and at the same time fashioned a revolution in public taste that was at least partly government sponsored.

More than anything, our public life was shaped, and occasionally distorted, by fears of Soviet aggression. And it was this fear that fuelled the most decisive change of the decade: the emergence of Canada as a branch-office nation, a handmaiden of the economy of the United States.

Looking back on my own adolescence in the 1950s, I occasionally wonder if there was anything I did or saw that was significant enough to capture the elusive flavour of that decade.

How about the crowd of shoppers standing in front of Mr. Mullins' radio store in New Westminster, British Columbia, one epochal afternoon in 1950. Mr. Mullins had erected the town's first television aerial on top of his store and managed to pull in a signal from Seattle that flickered impressively on the screen he had set up in his display window. Today, after reading McLuhan, I realize that I was witnessing the birth of a "new order of electronic priorities, stimulated by a multi-sensory media mix." At the time, though, all I saw in Mr. Mullins' window was an undulating, snow-flecked image of a puppet show called "Howdy Doody," which prompted my father to comment that he'd be damned if he'd be caught buying one of those things, especially at the price Mullins was asking.

And what is there to say about the beautiful Sunday afternoon that the Korean War began. Our family was driving down to Crescent Beach, and when the news came through on the car radio, the announcer's voice carried an urgency that made me understand something important had happened. The sun that day was hot and the water

The smiling face of the B-A *man was familiar to motorists in the fifties.*

Opposite page: *During the fifties, everything grew up. Grocery stores became supermarkets and two-lane roads matured into superhighways.*

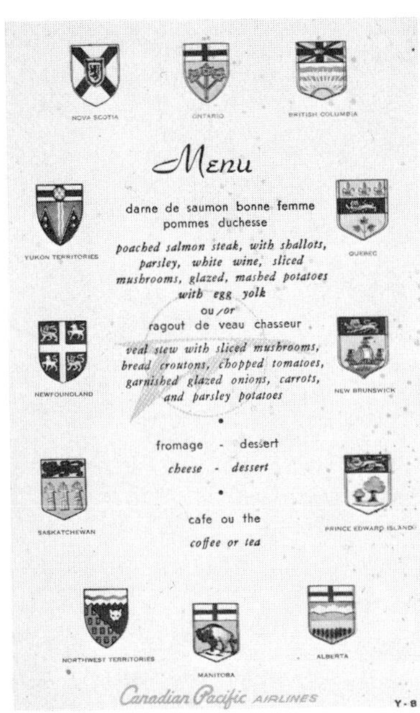

In 1959, CPA inaugurated a daily flight from Vancouver to Montreal, stopping at Winnipeg and Toronto. This CPA menu reflects a tradition of excellence in mid-air dining.

was warm. I swam and lay down on a wet towel in the sun and later we had chicken salad for supper and listened to the "Hour of Charm" on the radio and talked in a desultory way about "what those Communists will do next." That question, as it turned out, was the one that shaped our public policies and our private lives more decisively than anything else in the 1950s. But at the time the question seemed casual and remote, like the weather on the other side of the country. It was, after all, a far-away war, and no one *we* knew was going to be fighting it.

giddy economic explosion

Or was it significant that, in the Phi Delta Theta house at the University of British Columbia in 1956, some of my fraternity brothers used to spend their lunch hours phoning their brokers. Today I can recognize it as a result of one of the giddiest economic explosions in Canadian history. At the time, I viewed it only as an impressive coincidence that a friend of mine could buy a bright red, wire-wheeled MG from the proceeds of a coup in Trans-Mountain Pipe Line stock.

And finally, do any cultural insights surface from my coffee-house-and-cool-jazz phase of the late 1950s. In those days, the music was improvised and unamplified, and our heroes were existential jazzmen like Charlie Parker and Lennie Tristano. Beatniks would gather in murky, white-washed basements full of candlelit tables, drink espresso coffee at fifty cents a cup and talk in low tones. Often, usually after midnight, there would be a progressive jazz group on the stand. Everyone would settle down as the band rode through the first thirty-two bars of one of the bop anthems ("Lullaby of Birdland," say, or "Bernie's Tune") and listen intently as the trumpet, trombone, sax and piano improvised their solos in turn. It was barely permissible to yell "Go, man, go!" during up-tempo solos, but even loud talking was frowned upon. And dancing was inconceivable. The music was not designed for it. Besides, dancing would not have been profound.

There was something intensely 1950s about this ritual of digging progressive jazz. The whole point of the music was the improvised solo, an act of unrehearsed, instantaneous creation. By attaching so much importance to the spontaneity of a creative act, we were paying homage to everything that is unique and instinctive in the individual.

Individuality was a principle that seemed to need defending in the 1950s. Everywhere we looked we saw the development of huge, impersonal structures: corporations, governments, power-blocs and mass markets.

Conformity was the big issue in those days, and no thoughtful undergraduate was in favour of it. The equation seemed delightfully simple. Working for IBM was conformist. Living in the suburbs was conformist. Progressive jazz was anti-conformist. White shirts for men were conformist. Black stockings for girls were anti-conformist, not to say beat. The world, as undergraduates viewed it, was divided into them and us. *Them* were people who worked for huge, soulless corporations; *us* were people who refused to knuckle under to the system. Most people, in other words, were squares. But some were hipsters, or hoped they were.

the giant statistic

It is easy to argue that this square-hipster split was simply another version of the endless clash between generations. It probably was, but I think as a response it also reflected something that was unique in the Canadian experience, something that provided the essential flavour of that troubled, turbulent, prosperous decade. The central fact was this: in the 1950s, we learned to live with bigness.

It was the decade of the giant statistic. Canada's gross national product rose from $18.4 billion in 1950 to $36.8 billion by the decade's end. The average weekly industrial wage, which was $45.08 when the decade began, rose to an unimaginable $73.47 by the end of the decade, and not much of the increase was caused by inflation. Our population increased by more than 4 million, one of the biggest jumps in any decade.

3,541,381 cars

During the 1950s we bought 3,541,381 passenger cars, built 1,115,485 new housing units (most of them suburban bungalows with big front lawns and picture windows) and produced more babies (exactly 4,322,904 of them, according to the Dominion Bureau of Statistics) than in any previous decade.

Statistics alone, however, cannot convey how this new scale of things – big growth, big money, big cities, big bombs – affected our daily lives. To begin with, we learned to live with the awesome prospect of instant extermination. This fear helped create much of the prosperity that changed our lives. Nearly all the major economic developments of the 1950s – Kitimat, Ungava iron ore, the St. Lawrence Seaway, the uranium boom – were either initiated or hastened by the cold war.

Even more decisive to our prosperity than the cold war was the simple fact that, after a decade of depression and another decade of war and postwar austerity, people wanted things. And for the first time since the 1920s, the things they wanted were available in quantity and large numbers of Canadians were in a position to buy them.

In the 1950s Canadians also discovered the mass market and their own uneasy role in it. The consumer revolution brought something new into the Canadian make-up: a sense of fun. With more leisure time and more money than ever before, Canadians learned the importance of being frivolous. Our fads and sports and off-hours activities, from curling to hula hoops to square dancing to rock 'n' roll, assumed a new importance in our lives. Teenagers, who had been regarded at the beginning of the decade simply as young adults, assumed a new importance too. For the first time, their fads, their styles and their pursuit of fun began to be emulated by other age groups.

consumer revolution

The handmaiden of this consumer revolution was television. The CBC introduced its service in 1952, although several hundred thousand Canadians living within range of American stations already owned sets. Before the end of the decade, the new medium had revolutionized Canadian life more profoundly than any invention since the mass-produced car. Family life, eating habits, house design, conversation, jokes, political attitudes, *everything* was transformed by television. Despite the woeful predictions of its critics, television did not depress mass taste. It may actually have helped to raise it, for the decade that discovered television also witnessed a significant cultural and educational boom in Canada.

The 1950s, in other words, was a decade of mass trends. There were some stirring events in Canada, but these were overshadowed by such things as television, immigration, and changing patterns of consumption – trends that changed our lives more decisively, and more swiftly, than all the headline-grabbing events of the entire decade.

By 1950, doctors at the Hospital for Sick Children in Toronto had developed a life-saving combination of antibiotics that saved one out of every two children stricken with tuberculous meningitis. Youngsters who once were expected to live six weeks were now returning to school.

CHAPTER ONE

The Emergence of Gaiety

Like most Canadians I'm indifferent to the visit of the Queen.

Joyce Davidson, 1959

The new decade came to a grey country in a grey time. In Sumas Prairie, twenty-eight miles southeast of Vancouver, melting snows had flooded hundreds of acres of farmland, and some homeowners spent the first hours of 1950 bailing out their living rooms. In St. John's, Newfoundland, police reported more drunkenness than usual and blamed it on people who used their family allowance cheques – unknown until the merger into Confederation the previous year – to buy screech.

In Toronto, a dense fog failed to keep partygoers off the freezing streets, and police arrested 103 of them for drunkenness. In Stratford, Ontario, in the early hours of the new decade, one man managed to steal fifty-four feet of a concrete-slab sidewalk by carting it off in sections. Near Schomberg, Ontario, 150 motorists spent six hours on the highway, stranded by freezing rain. At midnight, they honked their horns in unison, a sad and defiant cacophony that was muffled by the swirling fog.

In Toronto, a civic election was scheduled for the following Monday, and a plebiscite on Sunday sports was the big issue. In pulpits across the city, the New Year's Day sermon was devoted to warnings of the evils of a pagan sabbath. If Toronto voted for Sunday sports, cautioned the pastor at Bonar Presbyterian Church, Sunday drinking would be next. "There is no length to which the liquor people will not go," added the Reverend B. Simpson Black, "to make more money by debauching the youth of this Dominion."

But most of the nation had debauched itself handily the night before – at house parties in Winnipeg, at Odd Fellows Halls in a thousand prairie whistle-stops, at night clubs in Vancouver where you kept the ginger ale on top of the table and the rye underneath, safely out of sight.

It was a celebration and a national ritual, but it was a peculiarly cheerless one. It was the cheerlessness of a nation that believed in work, revered authority and mistrusted pleasure and all the gentler arts, a state of sensibility that some commentators still sneeringly describe as "Victorian." But that adjective suggests a certain florid opulence that the Canada of 1950 did not possess. Across more than four thousand miles, no public building of architectural merit had been erected for at least twenty years. There were probably fewer than a score of restaurants in the entire country that a European would consider adequate. Visiting opera companies performed in hockey arenas because the nation did not possess a single adequate concert hall outside Toronto and Montreal. When a Montreal sculptor named Robert

Jack Kent Cook's Canadian Liberty *sold glamour in the popular style. Although most of the articles were U.S. in content, Canadian stars sometimes made the magazine's cover.*

***Opposite page:** Dressed in their Sunday best, Ottawa schoolchildren cheer the Princess in 1951.*

Roussil carved an abstract form from a poplar tree, entitled it *Peace* and displayed it outside a Montreal gallery, police charged him with violating a local obscenity by-law and a righteous citizen used a four-by-four timber to clobber off what looked like the statue's head.

Our national aspirations were equally modest. Most Canadians seemed to share the conviction that Canada was a second-rate country. Our allegiance, our livelihood, our love of the land were Canadian, but most of our notions of excellence and nobility, most of our aspirations toward affluence and success, most of our national myths came from somewhere else.

Mostly, of course, they came from Britain. The conventional wisdom had it that Britain was, on the whole, the wisest, bravest, most noble, most generous, most humane country the world had ever seen. This assessment, although it happened to be true to quite a surprising extent, hardly enhanced our own sense of nationhood. We were expected to be proud not so much of our Canadian institutions, but of their British origin.

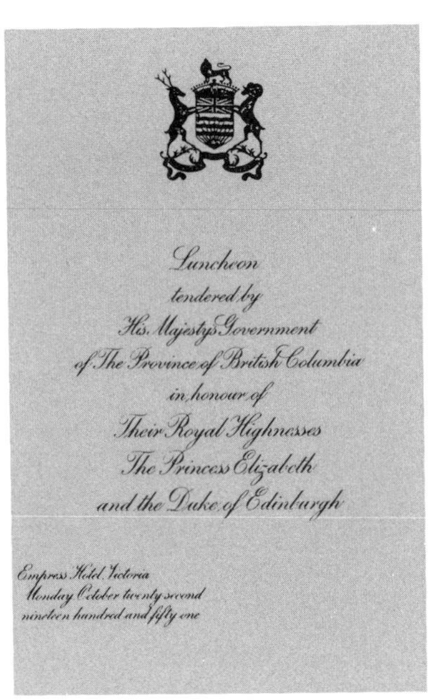

Luncheon
tendered by
His Majesty's Government
of The Province of British Columbia
in honour of
Their Royal Highnesses
The Princess Elizabeth
and the Duke of Edinburgh

Empress Hotel Victoria
Monday October twenty second
nineteen hundred and fifty one

At Victoria's Empress Hotel H.R.H. and guests lunched on Smoked Salmon aux Caprès and Noisettes of Spring Lamb. Guests were told what to wear, what to say and when to say it. On the morning of the luncheon, government staff handled a hundred calls, mostly from women who wanted to know if their dress was appropriate for the occasion.

enter Mr. Justice Chevrier

This attitude was admirably expressed in the early 1950s by Mr. Justice Edgar Rudolphe Eugene Chevrier, of the Supreme Court of Ontario. Justice Chevrier was a zealot about British justice. He refused to allow new words such as "okay" or "hospitalization" in his court. He persuaded his brother justices to swap their plain black robes for gowns of royal blue with red and black collars, red sashes and long mauve cuffs. At assizes, he insisted on being preceded into court by a sheriff bearing a sword, in accordance with ancient British ritual. He actually persuaded some court officials to wear cutaway coats with lace ruffles and lace cuffs. "The matter of wigs was also discussed," the judge once confessed, "but I had to compromise."

Coast to Coast with H.R.H.

In 1951 the fairytale Princess of countless magazine and newspaper pieces toured Canada with her Greek prince charming, Philip. In '57 she returned as the Queen, and in '59 opened the St. Lawrence Seaway.

Sou'westered and gum-booted, Princess Elizabeth viewed Niagara Falls, Canada's attraction for honeymooners and dignitaries.

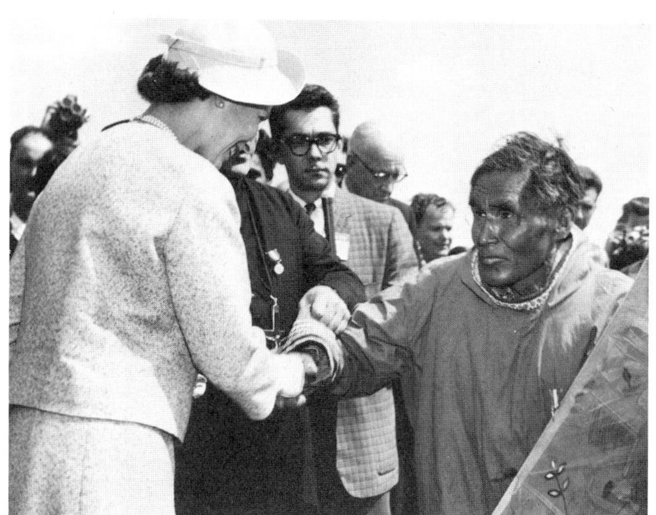

An unusual gift for a Queen: two beaded moose-skin jackets from Nescaupee Chief, Willy Einsh, at Schefferville, Quebec.

Another bouquet, this one from Newfoundland Premier Joey Smallwood's grand-daughter during the Queen's visit in 1959.

Most of Judge Chevrier's countrymen apparently shared his love of British tradition. When the future Queen of England and her consort arrived in Canada in October 1951, for the first postwar royal visit, they triggered an outpouring of emotion that had not been equalled in Canada since V-E Day. Part of the enthusiasm was inspired by simple curiosity; Elizabeth and Philip were still the world's best-known newly-weds. Mainly, however, the warmth of their greeting was inspired by an unabashed love of England, the country we had so recently helped to defend. In honouring the princess and her husband, Canadians were honouring all that was best in their own country, and in themselves. It was a glorious tour by a great lady among a grateful people.

It was also the last occasion of its kind, for the country was changing, imperceptibly but swiftly. The stability, the traditional moral values and the old colonial ties that the monarchy exemplified were being undermined by a newer way of life: the life-style of the cities, the morality of the technological age and the new permissiveness of the postwar generation.

the new permissiveness

Canada's story for the rest of the decade was largely one of isolated skirmishes between the majority of Canadians who wanted to divert themselves in an appropriately urban manner, and the vocal minority who attempted to prevent them from doing so. For the first time since the 1920s, the laws and customs regulating public morality were under serious pressure from a population whose values were changing. As urbanization, the automobile and the mass media disseminated the gospel of the new permissiveness, the guardians of public morality suddenly found themselves on the losing side. A society that was less structured, more mobile and more affluent than ever before

A programme for the Queen's review of Toronto's 48th Highlanders.

Sunday Sport Sparks Row in Fiery Debate at Church

The Globe and Mail, 1950

Sunday Sports Okayed Backers Demand Action

Toronto Daily Star, 1950

Baseball Likely First Sunday Sports Fare

Toronto Daily Star, 1950

This sample of newspaper headlines (above and opposite page) indicates the controversy surrounding Sunday sports and alcohol during the decade.

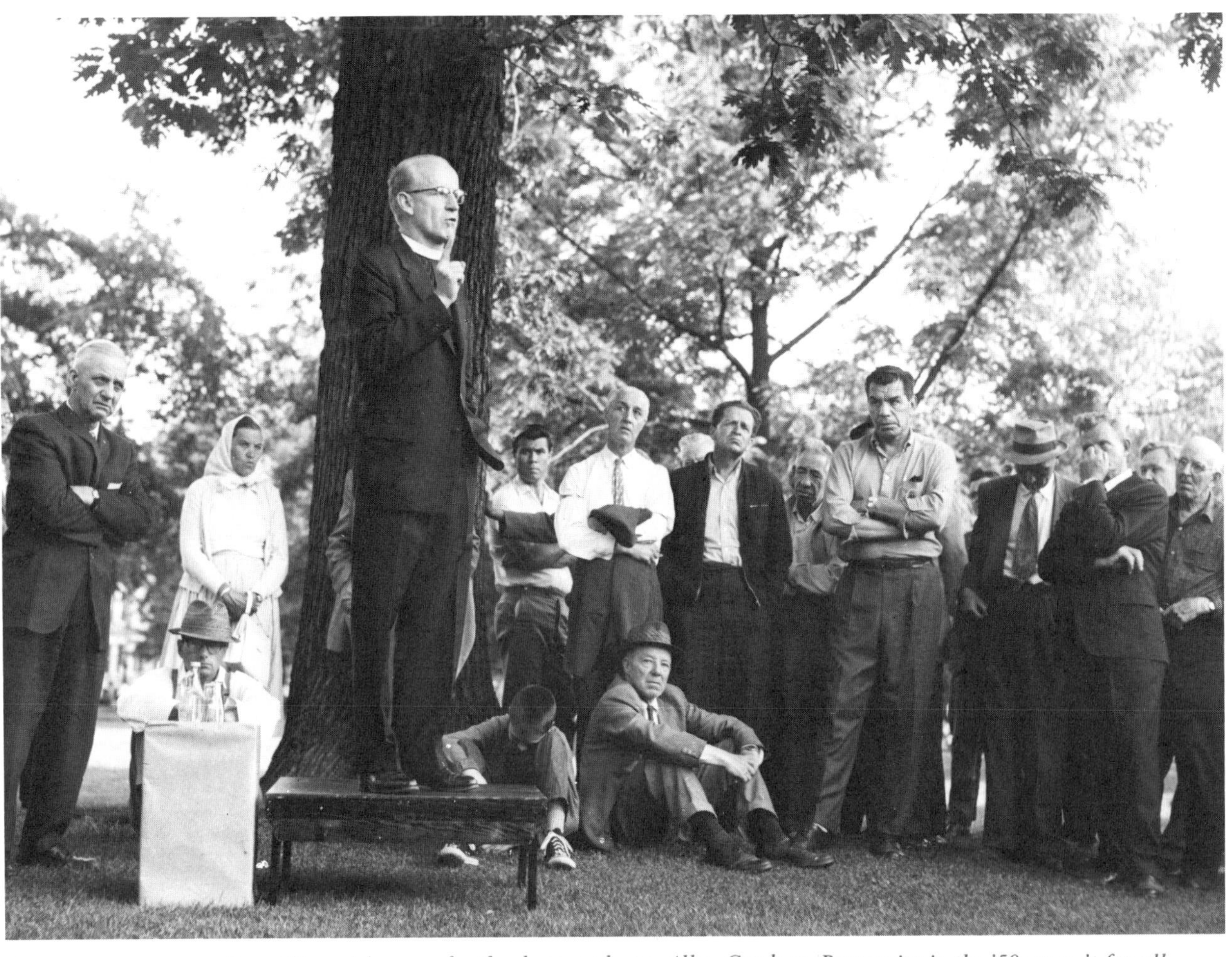

A street-corner evangelist at Toronto's oasis for the down-and-out, Allan Gardens. Prosperity in the '50s wasn't for all.

began to realize that it was entitled to more freedom and more fun. By the end of the 1950s it got it, but not without a fight.

Most of the skirmishing centred around the liquor laws of the ten provinces. These jurisdictions earned more than $219 million from liquor in 1950, and they spent a fair proportion of it ensuring that the liquor they sold was consumed under conditions that were as unattractive as possible. In most provinces, public consumption of hard liquor was illegal, except in certain private clubs, where magistrates could often be seen relaxing with a legal highball after a hard day sentencing liquor offenders. Ordinary Canadians either bought their hard liquor at a government store and drank it at home or took their bottle to a nightclub or dancehall and kept it under the table.

The lower orders drank beer – an estimated 181 gallons in 1950 – in surroundings which, since they are fast disappearing, are worth describing for posterity. The Canadian beer parlour was nearly always located in a hotel, which nearly always

Everyone's attention was focussed on the tiny TV screen in the corner of this St. Catherine Street bar in Montreal.

Sides Change in Canada's Liquor Battle

The Financial Post, 1959

Just Who Are "Dry" Forces?

The Financial Post, 1959

Alcohol Real Money Maker For Canada's Governments

The Financial Post, 1959

existed for the sole purpose of selling beer. It was nearly always furnished with tiny, circular tables and chromium-tubing chairs. The walls were nearly always painted a pale, institutional green, and the floor was nearly always covered with linoleum or ceramic tiles of the sort that ornamented public-school washrooms of the 1940s. It was nearly always full of men, shouting to be heard above the din from the reverberating walls, the slamming of wet glasses on formica tabletops and the shouts of hurrying waiters. And since there was nearly always nothing else to do but drink beer – music and snacks were nearly always forbidden – the patrons were nearly always quite drunk. This was how English-speaking Canada drank in the early 1950s.

The province of Quebec, and Montreal in particular, gloried in cocktail bars, beer and wine with meals and licensed nightclubs. Elsewhere, the nation was a patchwork of ancient laws that failed to discourage drinking, but succeeded magnificently in encouraging drunkenness.

The Law and How It's Broken: There's No National Pattern

The Financial Post, 1959

In all of Saskatchewan and Manitoba, there was no place where a woman could legally drink in public, apart from a few private clubs. In Calgary and Edmonton, men and women were allowed to drink in separate beverage rooms, but not together. Victoria had been dry since 1924, and in 1950 voted to stay that way, at least until the next referendum. In Alberta, anyone who bought a bottle at the government store and failed to go home by the most direct route was technically guilty of a violation that could result in a jail term. In Prince Edward Island, even shaving lotion was banned by the Temperance Commission, and store owners were occasionally hauled into court for having it on their shelves. Most medium-sized cities had "blind pigs," illegal taverns which usually operated with police co-operation. Others got around the law with "private" clubs that handed out memberships to anyone with the price of admission.

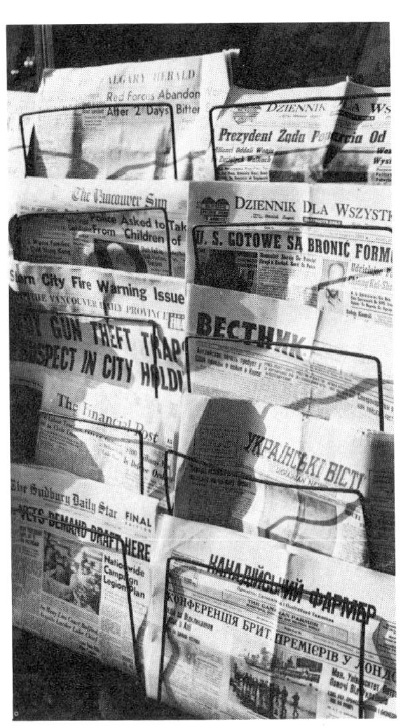

The lure of Canada hit its peak in 1957 when in a single year almost 300,000 immigrants made their homes here. Although a quarter of all post-war "new Canadians" were from Great Britain, the influx from non-English-speaking countries rapidly changed the character of most Canadian cities. This Sudbury newsstand displayed only a few of the papers that chronicled world news for multi-lingual Canada.

the forces of public purity

It was plain that the climate had to change. A Gallup poll indicated that more than 70 per cent of the population were drinkers. Slowly, the message filtered through to politicians that if they reformed the blue laws, they would gain more votes than they would lose.

One by one, the provinces cracked. British Columbia authorized cocktail lounges and licensed restaurants in 1953, and the urban landscape suddenly blossomed with dozens of dimly lit, chrome-and-leather cocktail bars, each with its own extravagant decor. In Manitoba, after cocktail bars opened in the spring of 1957, Winnipeg police reported a decline in boot-legging and "less drunkenness and fewer loose characters hanging around." This was not an isolated phenomenon. The morning after Edmontonians were allowed to patronize cocktail bars for the first time in thirty-five years, not a single drunk turned up on the docket in magistrate's court, something that court officials could not recall ever having happened before. For the first time, the forces of public purity began to seem irrelevant, even to politicians.

By the end of the decade, Canadian blue laws had eroded to the vanishing point, and their supporters had become a dwindling band of well-intentioned ladies who talked mainly to each other. When last heard of, temperance advocates in Nova Scotia were urging the government to banish pickled eggs from beverage rooms.

rise in immigration

The liberalization of our drinking laws was paralleled, and perhaps influenced by, a rise in immigration. Exactly 1,544,642 immigrants, mostly from Europe, settled in Canada during the decade. Only about 300,000 of them were from the United Kingdom; and in the ten years following the war, at least 60,000 returned to Britain. Most of the others came from places like Poland, Hungary, southern Italy, the Ukraine, Holland and Germany. By the middle of the decade, the number of Canadians of British origin had declined from 50 to 46 per cent.

The influence of this new, non-British majority was being felt in countless ways. In Toronto, where the Italian community numbered just under 140,000 by the end of the decade, lasagna and exotic foreign cheeses became staples in supermarkets. A man with the flagrantly Ukrainian name of Hawrelak was elected mayor of Edmonton, and another named Juba became mayor of Winnipeg. In Vancouver, German immigrants opened so many stores selling sauerkraut, Telefunken radios, Hamburg sausage and *Der Spiegel,* that the downtown street where most of them were located became known as Robsonstrasse. By the late 1950s, older residents who once complained of the

NEVER ON SUNDAYS

by NORRIS

The daily cartoon from the pointed pen of Len Norris was an experience to be savoured, like afternoon tea in Victoria. Those laughing loudest were often the next day's offering.

"I said . . . if they try this Lord's Day Act business on our Sunday Symphony, Sidney will certainly give them an earful . . ."

". . . and now, my good man, could I trouble you for two small cocktail glasses?"

"We'll start with the old tried and true. Complimentary copies to all public officials to assure good burning and banning publicity. . ."

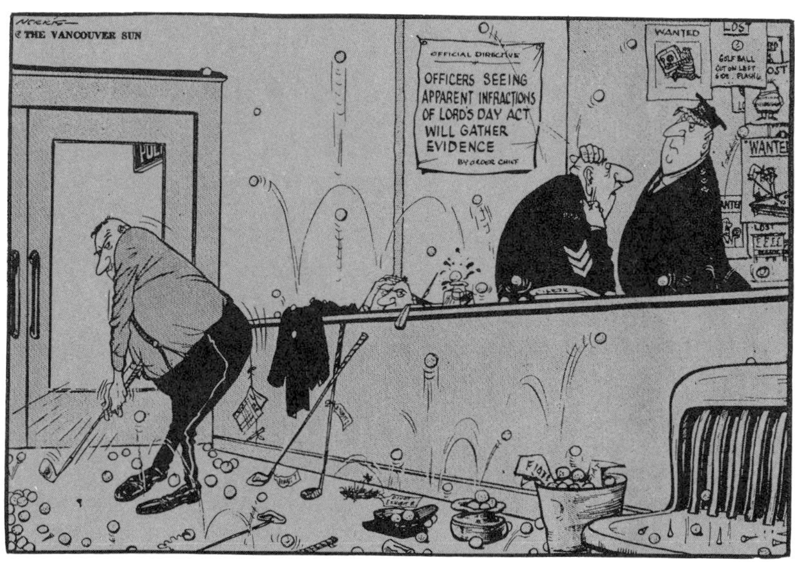

"Finnigan was gathering evidence, became infatuated with the game, been practising ever since for next year's Canadian Open . . ."

influx of "DPs" could be found boasting to visitors about how cosmopolitan their cities had become.

By 1958, a Canadian of German descent named John Diefenbaker was calling for a new approach to national unity that he dubbed "unhyphenated Canadianism." He underlined his point by naming an Indian to the Senate and a Canadian of Ukrainian descent to his cabinet. For good measure, he also named Ellen Fairclough Canada's first woman cabinet minister. His actions were reported to the readers of *Maclean's,* Canada's national magazine, by a "Czech-born" journalist named Peter C. Newman.

In this heady atmosphere, it is hardly surprising that the prevailing attitudes to sex changed along with everything else. When the second Kinsey Report was published in 1953, it provoked the same shocked outcry in Canada as it did elsewhere in North America. Dr. Gordon Bates, general director of the Health League of Canada and the country's leading campaigner against venereal disease, described the report as "a statistical saturnalia" that could have devastating effects on the young. But Canadians bought thousands of hardcover copies of *Sexual Behavior in the Human Female,* and not all of them found it as shocking as did Dr. Bates.

By the end of the 1950s, girls in bikinis seldom attracted crowds, rude remarks or policemen, but Canadian swimwear manufacturers still pitched

Ellen Fairclough

Canada's first woman federal cabinet minister, Ellen Fairclough "threw her hat" into the federal arena in 1950. Before her parliamentary debut, she worked as a Public Accountant in her native Hamilton where she became known for her strong views and flamboyant millinery. Her 1957 appointment as Secretary of State in the Diefenbaker administration was a political breakthrough for the fifty-two-year-old mother and all women in public service.

The drive-in fifties—even the faithful could catch the Sunday morning sermon in the comfort of their own motorboats.

their bikini advertising toward girls who wanted to sunbathe in private. The new highrise apartment blocks that climbed Mount Royal, engulfed Toronto's St. George Street and transformed Vancouver's West End were invaded by crowds of eligible young people who lived and partied at close quarters. It was the beginning of the swingles phenomenon, although it would not be called that until the following decade. Shifts in moral standards are notoriously averse to precise measurement, and it is possible that the new permissiveness was more apparent than real. But whether or not there was more sex in the nation's bedrooms, there was certainly more of it in print. The introduction of *Playboy* magazine in 1953 expanded the frontiers of printed permissiveness in the United States and begat an entire new generation of prurient periodicals which inevitably slopped over the undefended border by the millions.

The sudden appearance of naked ladies on the newsstands gave the righteous a new cause, and they pursued it as zealously as they had fought cocktail bars a decade earlier. In Ontario in 1955, eleven thousand Catholic women launched what they called a Decency Crusade and visited every newsstand from Georgian Bay to Lake Erie in an attempt to pressure dealers into withdrawing objectionable material. Montreal passed a by-law regulating skin exposure on paperback covers. The Senate formed a Committee on Salacious and

Marilyn Reddick

For one year Miss Canada 1952 rode in convertibles, dined with dignitaries and millionaires and posed alongside politicians. She was flown to London for the Coronation, rode an ostrich at the Sportsman's Show, fell through a trap door on the *Magnificent* while entertaining Canadian troops and was photographed with Marilyn Monroe, her look-alike. She grossed $8,000 and felt she earned every cent. A disillusioned Marilyn Reddick passed the crown to her successor with neither tears nor regrets.

Modelling students in white gloves and hats caught the attention of lunch-time strollers in narrow lapels and cuffed pants.

Indecent Literature. In Quebec City in 1956, a group of about fifteen masked men descended on newsstands around town, tore up whatever displeased them and left leaflets warning each proprietor that they would be back unless he cleaned up his magazine rack.

Princess Margaret and Antony Armstrong-Jones

Hers was the love story of the fifties. Would Princess Margaret marry the man she loved and break royal convention? Her suitor, Peter Townsend, was fifteen years her senior, a divorced father of two children, and a commoner. The tabloid press had a field day. But Margaret renounced him for the crown. In 1960 she married a commoner, handsome photographer Antony Armstrong-Jones. Sixteen years later, their separation was announced and the marriage was over.

public burning at Lakehead

Gradually, of course, the censors moved on to other targets. Vladimir Nabokov's *Lolita* was banned from the Windsor Public Library. At the Lakehead, the citizenry held a public burning of D.H. Lawrence's *Lady Chatterley's Lover* and Fort William's mayor Catherine Seppala, who hadn't read it, called it "a dirty, rotten piece of filth." Dr. J.R. Mutchmor, Chairman of the United Church's Board of Evangelism and Social Service, was a more dutiful crusader. He bought a copy of Grace Metalious' *Peyton Place* in Buffalo, smuggled it into Canada (where it was banned) and read it. Then, on the train to Ottawa, where he was going to oppose an application that the ban be lifted, he read it a second time "to refresh my memory."

The machinery of censorship gradually slowed down however. Despite Dr. Mutchmor's protestations, *Peyton Place* was allowed into the country, although its readers commonly covered their copies with plain brown paper lest they be publicly identified as consumers of smut. Marlon Brando's *The Wild One,* though it was banned in Alberta and British Columbia in 1954 as a "revolting, sadistic story of degeneration," helped create a cult of would-be nihilists in black leather jackets. *Playboy* was allowed into the country in the summer of 1957; by that fall, its nude foldouts were adorning dormitory walls across the country.

Finance Minister Donald Fleming, who had been an influential member in the Upper Canada Bible Society, eventually transferred the duty of reviewing such objectionable imports from the federal tariff board to the courts. This was an eminently appropriate decision, for Canadians by this time had realized the absurdity of customs officials vetting their reading matter.

You could almost describe it as an act of self-assertion, this new Canadian unwillingness to subject private morals to the scrutiny of public authority. And the new attitude may have been reflected in our changing response to all authority, including the monarchy. When Queen Elizabeth flew to Ottawa in October, 1957, for a brief visit prior to her American tour, her reception was very different from the one we had extended only six years before. It is true that about 200,000 people gathered on Parliament Hill to see the Queen, in coronation robes and jewelled crown, drive past in an open carriage. It is also true that when her image appeared on the television screen in Victoria's Union Club, the entire room rose as one man to acknowledge her electronic presence. But it was a wan contrast to the previous royal visit.

"God Save The Queen"

A few weeks before her arrival, the Gallup poll revealed that only four out of ten Canadians were pleased with the news that she had consented to open Parliament. Another poll, conducted by *Canadian High News,* suggested that only one teenager in fifty approved of "God Save the Queen" as Canada's national anthem. On the day of her arrival, excursion trains from Montreal that had been scheduled especially for the visit arrived half-empty.

Her subsequent tour of the United States was, by contrast, a triumph. A million people waited in the rain to see her in Washington, and crowds lined almost every foot of the fifty-five-mile route into Virginia. Compared to this, Ottawa's greeting seemed lukewarm, and many newspapers said so.

When television personality Joyce Davidson observed on an American television programme that Canadians did not care much about royal tours any more, her remarks stirred quite a controversy. On balance, however, it seemed that many Canadians agreed with her.

It was true. The whole royalist mystique – the corgis, the newsreels of royal outings, the Christmas messages and the manufactured frenzy of royal visits – all of it was out of step with the urbanized country we had become.

an outrageous wink

Appropriately enough, it was a big-city Canadian girl named Sandra Seagram who certified the passing of the old order. Sandra, a vivacious Montreal blonde, was among 112 Canadian debutantes who were presented at Buckingham Palace in the summer of 1958. It was the last such presentation, for the palace had decided to replace it the following year with a series of less exclusive garden parties. Under the watchful eye of Mrs. Fiorenza Drew, wife of the Canadian High Commissioner, Sandra made her curtsey along with the rest, and then, in a gesture that made all the best Fleet Street gossip columns the next day, turned to Prince Philip and gave him a wholly unauthorized, entirely outrageous wink.

It was a beautiful moment. The gesture was humorous, cocksure, friendly, even a bit sexy – the very qualities that Philip himself was bringing to the monarchy. It symbolized, perhaps better than anything, the end of the grey Canada we had known, and the emergence of a new quality that only the very best nations possess: a sense of gaiety.

While PM Diefenbaker worried about the declining respect for the monarchy, Bay Street ticker-tape showered down on Queen Elizabeth and Prince Philip on July 29, 1959.

Royal Nostalgia

Royalty was big business in the booming fifties, and manufacturers put royal images on everything from china milk pitchers to soft drink bottle caps. There were so many things to commemorate – two royal children, three royal visits and the Coronation itself. Although some souvenirs lacked the craftsmanship for royal endorsement, these items occupied a special place in Canadian homes.

Every schoolgirl kept a scrapbook.

Canada Dry's royal bottle cap.

A gilt-edged Royal Doulton plate.

Nelson's view of the Coronation.

To toast Her Majesty's health.

An enamelled brass lapel pin.

A cast-brass decanter top.

Enthroned by George Weston Ltd.

OXO packaged its bouillon cubes in a regally decorated Coronation tin.

A Coronation decal, to be placed on the window of the store or family car.

His and Hers pressed tin plates, to be hung over the mantle in the rec room.

H.R.H. on a painted biscuit tin.

A non-commercial ad from O'Keefe's.

A package of Coronation bubble gum.

For smokers, a china cigarette box.

A Royal Visit teacup and saucer.

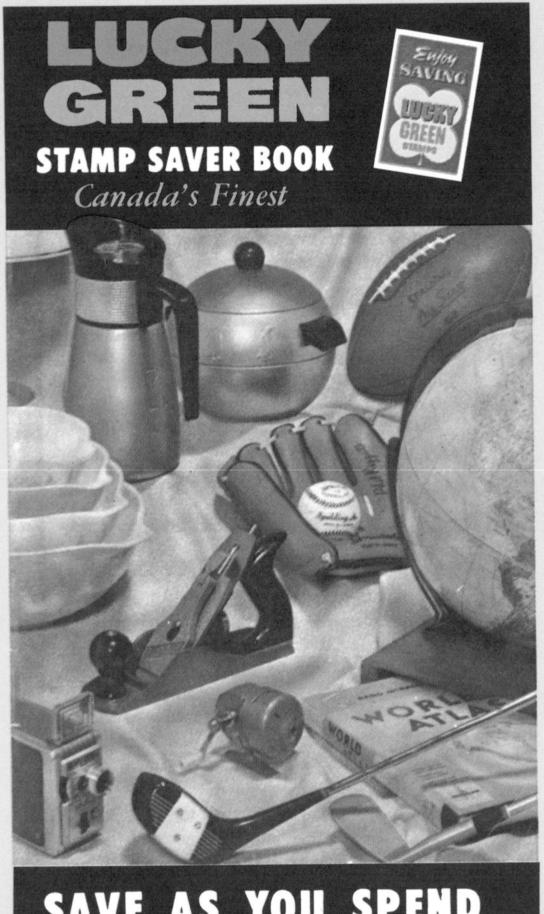

LUCKY GREEN
STAMP SAVER BOOK
Canada's Finest
Enjoy SAVING
LUCKY GREEN STAMPS
SAVE AS YOU SPEND

Gold Bond, Lucky Green, Domino and Pinky Stamps were the weekly dole at supermarket check-out counters. Consumers received one stamp for every 10¢ of the total purchase, and complete books of stamps could be redeemed for any gadget on the market. A chenille bedspread cost five books, a brand new electric shaver ten books, and a trip to Europe, air fare only, cost 322 books, only!

CHAPTER TWO

More Money, More Pleasures

Don't just stand there, buy something!

"Honest Ed" Mirvish

Consider some of the wonderful gadgets that we discovered with pleasure and quickly learned to take for granted in the 1950s. They nearly all seemed commonplace, but their cumulative effect may have been far greater than the effect of, say, the French Revolution on the average Frenchman. Urbanization, mass marketing and new technologies determined what happened when we got up in the morning, decided what we would eat, influenced the way we spent the hours between supper and bedtime and transformed the way our senses experienced this new but still familiar world.

The list is awesome: transistor radios, drip-dry shirts, contoured bedsheets, power lawnmowers, Volkswagens, tomatoes wrapped in cellophane, cameras with built-in exposure meters, aerosol cans, automatic washers and dryers, TV dinners, coloured Kleenex, portable barbecues, electric can-openers, Scrabble sets, portable electric typewriters, eye-level ovens, radiant heating, coloured telephones, paint-by-number kits, high fidelity, hair spray and instant cake mix. And big things too: hundreds of square miles of suburban houses; millions of new cars, most of them festooned with chrome trim, or breast-shaped bumper guards, or penile radiator ornaments or massive tail-fins; hundreds of miles of superhighways and spaghetti-like interchanges; scores of shopping plazas and supermarkets, laundromats and gas stations, suburban A-frame churches and downtown skyscrapers; Muffler Cities and Hamburger Havens.

Canadians in the 1950s began drifting away from the old production-centred values of thrift and caution and learned to live with mass affluence and mass leisure. We remained a hard-working nation, but the shift to the cities and the new technologies that we were finally able to afford turned us from a nation of producers into a nation of consumers.

This trend was best reflected in the sheer numbers of the postwar move to the cities. Canada's population increased by more than 4 million between 1951 and 1961. In this same period, the population of cities with 100,000 or more people increased by 4.6 million. The rural population, by contrast, grew hardly at all, and the number of people living in small towns (under 30,000 people) actually declined.

The automobile population grew even faster. We started the decade owning about 2 million cars. By 1956, there were almost as many cars as there were homes with indoor plumbing. In that same year, Canadians bought well over 400,000 new cars and scrapped 151,000 old ones. By 1960,

Duz, Dash and Dreft in the economy size, frozen TV dinners and large tubes of chlorophyll toothpaste filled consumers' shopping carts.

THE COST OF LIVING

Sample weekly budgets compiled by *Maclean's* in 1950 showed how a family of four might spend their money. The average wage: $45.08!

Net Income $45

Item	Amount	%
Food	$18.00	40%
Rent or Home Expense	7.50	16.5
Fuel and Light	2.25	5
Clothing	5.75	13
Home Furnishings, Repairs	2.25	5
Medical Care	2.25	5
Personal Care	1.50	3.25
Transportation	1.50	3.25
Recreation, Advancement	2.00	4.5
Insurance and Savings	2.00	4.5
	$45.00	100%

Net Income $60

Item	Amount	%
Food	$20.00	33%
Rent or Home Expense	9.50	16
Fuel and Light	3.25	5.5
Clothing	6.50	11
Home Furnishings, Repairs	4.50	7.5
Medical Care	3.50	6
Personal Care	2.00	3
Transportation	2.25	3.5
Recreation, Advancement	3.50	6
Insurance and Savings	5.00	8.5
	$60.00	100%

Net Income $80

Item	Amount	%
Food	$22.00	27.5
Rent or Home Expense	13.50	17
Fuel and Light	3.50	4.5
Clothing	8.50	10.5
Home Furnishings, Repairs	5.50	7
Medical Care	4.00	5
Personal Care	2.50	3
Transportation	2.50	3
Recreation, Advancement	8.00	10
Insurance and Savings	10.00	12.5
	$80.00	100%

we were driving more than 4 million cars, one for every 4.3 persons.

We did not regard these vehicles simply as appliances, either. When the automobile was still a badge of success, a means of achieving mobility and, according to the motivational researchers, a symbol of sexual potency, we cared about cars intensely. Teenagers counted the days until their sixteenth birthday, when they would be eligible to learn to drive. Older adolescents worshipped the Kalifornia Kustom Kar and spent hundreds of dollars resculpturing old jalopies (the favourite was the '32 Ford) into chrome-and-lacquer mechanical fantasies.

introducing the 1958 Edsel

In the suburbs, when someone bought a new car, small knots of people would gather to peer in the windows, kick the tires and solemnly debate the merits of the '52 Monarch versus the '52 Ford. The fall announcements of the new models from Detroit were occasions for genuine excitement, and the subject of a million coffee-break conversations. "The modern car," said the Canadian Automobile Association in 1956, "is part of the Canadian way of life, with Canadians convinced that owning a motor vehicle is a basic right."

Detroit did its best to persuade everybody to exercise this right. It was the heyday of planned obsolescence and of cars that had to be longer, heavier, faster and more ornate than the model of the year before. The 1946 Studebaker, with its breast-shaped steering wheel hub, its black-light dashboard controls and a shape that inspired radio comedians to joke that you could not tell whether it was going backward or forward was an international sensation. Detroit designers tried all through the decade to duplicate its success. In the process, they created a succession of cars that, in addition to being tinny, under-engineered, costly to repair and less than safe, were very nearly obscene to look at.

The trend had to end sometime, and it was probably Ford's introduction of the Edsel in 1958 that did most to restore common sense to automotive design. The Edsel was the best-researched car in history, and the influence of motivational research was embarrassingly apparent in the design of its radiator grill, which inspired dozens of unprintable jokes. The Edsel was a resounding flop, and from that moment Detroit began to reconsider. There were counter-trends that also encouraged the development of more sensible cars. Small Volkswagens and Austins had been gaining popularity in Canada since the early 1950s, and the mid-decade boom in imported sports cars, especially MGs, Austin Healeys and Triumphs, convinced thousands of motorists that cars did not have to resemble tanks. Detroit began to design compacts, and the era of the family sports car was on its way.

The sheer cost of all this short-lived machinery gave social commentators plenty to chew on, but the cars themselves were not the only price we paid for our love affair with the automobile. We also had to contend with the consequences of driving too many cars in cities that were not designed for them. The traffic jam thus became one of the great symbols of the 1950s.

traffic jams

Before urban planning caught up with the growth in the automobile population, it was a problem of awesome dimensions. Some planners enjoyed predicting the day would come when the downtown traffic flow, which had already slowed to a crawl as congestion increased, would simply stop entirely. The costs of relieving the problem, said the Canadian Federation of Mayors and Municipalities, "are of such magnitude that even

Toronto Goes Underground

Toronto tried moving people instead of cars with the first subway in Canada in 1954. The $54 million construction project (above) ran along Yonge Street. Executives got off at King station and shoppers at Queen. Fare was 10 cents.

the most imaginative project for the future conquest of space seems insignificant by comparison." That was almost an understatement. By 1958, Canadian governments were spending $1 billion a year on new roads, and still had not caught up with the automotive birthrate.

The traffic jams that Canadian motorists faced every day in the mid-1950s were truly unforgettable. Imperial Oil researchers discovered that the average motorist in Toronto had to drive nine miles to work, and it took him fifty minutes to get there. In Winnipeg, when a bridge closed for repairs in the summer of 1957, the line of stalled traffic stretched for six miles. In Calgary, some downtown firms offered to pay half the cost of lunch for employees who left their cars at home, and special "pennant bus" runs were established to ferry commuters from the downtown fringes to the city centre. In Vancouver, similar schemes were occasionally attempted, but nothing, including improved public transportation, could keep motorists from driving downtown.

a bungalow in the suburbs

In Montreal, where more than 300,000 cars were funnelled daily across a few narrow bridges onto an island of narrow streets, the problem was worst of all. Police estimated in 1957 that one out of eight Montreal drivers parked illegally. The installation of a single traffic light caused jams that took several hours to unsnarl. The situation was so bad, the Federation of Mayors and Municipalities told the Gordon Commission on Canada's economic prospects, that the time saved by the introduction of the shorter work week "has been largely offset by the increased time spent transporting the average person from home to work and back."

Increasingly, that home tended to be a new bungalow in the suburbs, with a large front lawn, a picture window, a semi-finished basement and enough room and grass and trees surrounding it to make most suburbanites thankful they had escaped the city. Suburbs were not regarded as part of the city, but as an alternative to it. Thus the suburbs that proliferated in the 1950s were not regarded as an aesthetic disgrace, but as the answer to a desperate need.

the "planned community"

For men who had fought a war and then returned to inadequate housing, a bungalow in the suburbs was not a reluctant compromise. It was the fulfilment of a dream. Between 1946 and 1954, a quarter of a million families became suburbanites, and most were thankful. "You wake up in the morning and there are trees all around you," one new resident of Bedford Basin, a suburb of Halifax, explained to a *Maclean's* reporter. "You can look out on the water, not on your neighbour's fence. It's quiet and the air is salty and pure. To hell with the city! It may have more conveniences, but not more advantages."

Since the need for housing was desperate, and since postwar Canadians regarded suburbia as a kind of peacetime utopia, the growth was explosive. Cities had been expanding all through the war years – our urban population jumped 30 per cent between 1941 and 1951 – but by the 1950s we began regarding this growth as a permanent condition, rather than a temporary aberration.

Toronto grew fastest of all, faster in fact than either Houston or Los Angeles, which were both cited as outstanding boom cities during the 1950s. In the first half of the decade, Toronto grew by at least fifty thousand people a year, creating a need for eight square miles of new housing annually. In five years, the United Church built twenty-six churches in the Toronto area and decided in 1956 that it needed twenty-seven more. The same year

Lynwood Heights
Agincourt
3-Bedroom Bungalows
NHA
$11,460
$2,510 CASH
Salary Requirement $3,600
1 NHA 5½% 25-YEAR MORTGAGE
MONTHLY PAYMENTS $55
ARCHITECT DESIGNED
PROFESSIONAL COLOR STYLE
LARGE LANDSCAPED LOT
BRICK AND STUCCO CONSTRUCTION
ALUMINUM WINDOWS
DIVIDED BASEMENT
COME DIRECT TO THE EAST SIDE OF KENNEDY RD., ¼ OF A MILE NORTH OF SHEPPARD AVE. CALL OX. 4090; EVGS., ZONE 2-859.
EXCLUSIVE AGENT
CLYDE DAVIES LIMITED
REAL ESTATE

Dozens of suburban developments sprang up like mushrooms on the outskirts of cities in the fifties. A three-bedroom bungalow cost $11,460 @ 5½% mortgage.

Bell Telephone, which had installed 160,000 new phones since 1951, still had a waiting list of thousands.

Land speculation made hundreds rich. A widow whose sixty-five-acre farm stood in the path of an encroaching Toronto suburb sold it in 1954 for $145,000. One year and two trades later, the same land changed hands for $395,000.

Postwar planners laid down stiff zoning regulations for new developments, thus inaugurating the era of the "planned community." By and large, the effort was successful. In Kitimat, British Columbia, in Toronto's Don Mills, in Winnipeg's Wildwood and Vancouver's Fraserview, developers grouped their houses into neighbourhoods that clustered around a school and were limited by natural boundaries such as main streets or parks. Essential services were installed first instead of last, and planners laid great stress on curving streets, buried telephone wires, variations in house plans and provision for orderly future growth. The houses were bigger too: an average of 1,200 square feet in 1957, compared with 839 square feet in 1947. To a proud new resident of Don Mills or Fraserview, gazing through his picture window upon a vista of parks, trees, manicured lawns and curving streets that were almost safe for children to play baseball on, the postwar millennium must have seemed almost within reach.

Don Mills and Fraserview

Even the people seemed different, for a new suburban ethos was emerging, and a freer, friendlier, healthier, more informal life-style. That's the way it seemed, for instance, to a chemical engineer who moved into a house in North York in 1954. "The night we moved in," his wife explained to a reporter, "I was tired to the point of tears, until our new nextdoor neighbour came over with some beer and sandwiches. Nobody ever did that for us

The magic phrase of the fifties was Real Estate. Thousands of agents from Vancouver to Halifax hung out their shingles and never looked back. Whether your dream was a cottage on the lake or a multi-million dollar shopping plaza, the name on the sign told you the person to call.

The Golden Mile, literally one mile of stores and supermarkets, boasted one-stop shopping for Toronto's eastern suburbs. Built

Remember the jokes about the Fuller Brush man? Well, one person took them seriously. By 1950 Alf Fuller of Nova Scotia had built a sixty-hour-a-week job peddling brushes door to door into a multi-million dollar business empire. The Fuller Brush Girl, *a movie made in 1950 starring Lucille Ball was a comedy hit of the decade.*

in the city."

Being neighbourly was part of the dream. So was getting back to the soil, as we can see from inspecting Simpson's catalogues. In 1951, one type of power mower was listed; by 1954, Simpson's offered eight brands. Sales of ornamental shrubs tripled in the ten postwar years. A stonemason in Ontario reported that for every outdoor barbecue he had built around 1945 he was building a hundred a decade later. "In over thirty-five years of business," added a butcher in Toronto's Bayview area, "I've never sold so many thick steaks."

No sooner had the grass begun to sprout in Don Mills and Fraserview, however, than a great anti-suburban reaction set in. Deploring tract housing became a national indoor sport. Too many of the houses, said the critics, were jerry-built. In Halifax, one would-be suburbanite who had been quoted a price of $13,000 for a new house discovered that his builder's only blueprints consisted of some sketches scrawled on the back of an envelope. In Montreal, the roof of one instant bungalow collapsed before the house was finished. Too much of the landscaping, said the critics, consisted of promises. In Toronto, the *Telegram* equipped reporters with four-wheel-drive jeeps to cover stories in the muddy suburbs. Residential architecture, said the critics, ran the gamut from anarchy to monotony.

Worst of all, said the critics – and some of the suburbanites agreed – was the pervasive, relentless, inescapable chumminess of suburban living. *Maclean's* magazine told of one man who painted his home a non-conformist shade of red, then went away for the weekend. When he returned, he found his suburban neighbours had gotten together to re-paint it a discreet grey with pastel trim, a colour-scheme that was more to their liking. "We found the suburbs were just one big blob of conformity," a suburban escapee told the Toronto *Star* in 1959. "There was such an aggressive, calculated spirit of friendliness, it was almost nauseating." Author Hugh Garner was another disgusted ex-suburbanite. He claimed that suspi-

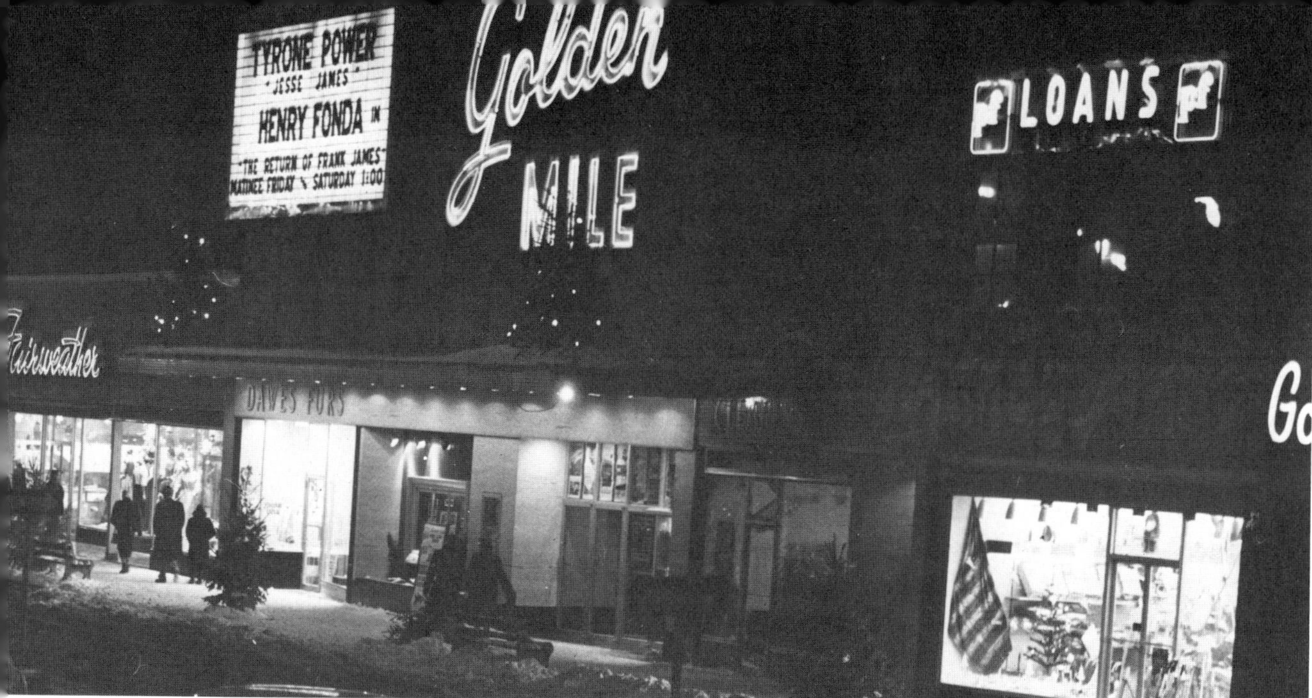

by the incredible Bennett brothers of Principal Investments, its construction signalled the end to many a neighbourhood store.

cious housewives in his neighbourhood used to time how long the laundryman spent inside their neighbours' houses.

The reaction against the suburbs was part of a bigger reaction against conformity, against being controlled and manipulated. We needed to react against it, because the 1950s was the first decade in which we felt threatened by organizations that existed primarily to sell us something. The long-awaited availability of a flood of consumer goods together with the affluence that made them affordable created an atmosphere in which almost everybody, one way or another, was a salesman, and those who weren't were at their mercy. Marketing, the new buzz-word for selling, became a national occupation, and consumption became a way of life.

You could see it along Toronto's Danforth Avenue where, by 1954, more than sixty used-car dealers had created a four-mile-long jungle of neon and floodlights, festooned with streamers and Buy Now signs and inhabited by a small army of commission salesmen who unloaded forty thousand cars a year. You could see it in the balance sheet of Principal Investments Limited, a Toronto firm that became Canada's biggest landlord by building shopping centres across the country and renting them to retailers in return for a percentage of sales.

The owners of Principal Investments, Archie, Jacob and David Bennett, helped orchestrate an event that almost became a Canadian ritual: the grand opening of the suburban shopping centre. When Lawrence Plaza opened in 1953, the festivities included clowns who gave away ten thousand packages of life-savers, drum majorettes who handed out special editions of the Toronto *Telegram,* college students dressed as giant Planter's peanuts who danced on the back of a flat-bed truck and models who passed out free candy and balloons. There were fireworks and square dancing in the vast parking lot for three nights running, two magicians, a ventriloquist, a draw for a new Ford, free transportation in chartered buses and an appearance by the 48th Highlanders Pipe Band.

Countless Canadian owners must have sworn at ads like this as they tried to coax life into their European import on cold winter mornings.

Although Vancouver opened the country's first drive-in bank in 1950, it was the Bennett Brothers who played host in 1954 to Canada's first drive-in church service. Somehow it seemed appropriate, for the shopping plaza was becoming the centre of worship of a new, secular religion.

There were other sales-promotion stunts that made the Bennetts' efforts look tame. Sunbeam Bread sponsored what they called the world's biggest picnic at the Canadian National Exhibition. One hundred thousand kids attended and collected more than half a million free comic books. To attract buyers to a new subdivision in Brampton, Ontario, the developers scattered 7,500 silver dollars over two hundred acres of subdivided land. A car dealer in Sherbrooke offered war-surplus airplanes as premiums to new-car buyers. Others offered mink stoles and television sets. In Victoria, one store sold chesterfields for 98 cents a pound. In Timmins, an appliance dealer offered to cut up a deer or elk for anyone who bought a home freezer.

Advertising in the fifties was a big, bold and up-front business. Beer and liquor firms capitalized on relaxed laws and abandoned their traditional soft-sell for a more direct pitch. By the end of the decade, Canada was #4 in per capita beer consumption.

TV dinners

Even the salesmen got incentives. In a single week in 1958, Dominion Dairies sent seventy-five top-selling Ontario milkmen and their wives to New York, O'Keefe Breweries sent six beer salesmen on an expense-paid Bermuda holiday and General Electric sent seventy dealers to Mexico.

It was not apparent while it was happening, but the new consumer-oriented life-style affected us in surprisingly basic ways. The custom of supper in the dining room virtually disappeared during the 1950s, for instance; a 1955 survey revealed that 70 per cent of the population ate all three meals in the kitchen. Ice cream consumption was four times above the level of the 1920s, consumption of frozen orange juice hit twenty million gallons by 1955, nearly one hundred varieties of TV dinners were on the market, and one-third of food-store buying was said to be done on impulse.

a gadget revolution

Affluence was abroad in the land, but not for everybody. Our new obsession with consumer goods made it easier to disguise the fact that Canada still had too many poor people. An hour's work bought less steak in 1950 than it did just after the war. Only three other cities in the world bought more Cadillacs per capita than Toronto, but it was still possible for broadcaster Kate Aitken to receive a letter from a woman pregnant with her sixth child offering it for adoption because she and her husband could not support it on his salary of $44 a week.

The average industrial wage in 1950, the year Miss Aitken received that letter, was $45.08 per week. Six years later, one out of five Canadian households still lacked indoor plumbing. That statistic did not matter much if you were broiling a two-inch steak on an outdoor barbecue. In fact, food prices were rising so much faster than wages that, in some parts of the country, stores selling nothing but horsemeat actually enjoyed a brief vogue.

Regardless of how it was distributed, however, the new affluence changed the face of Canada. It affected our values, our morals, our digestion, our living rooms, our cities, our waistlines, our jobs, our schools, our tastes, our leisure time and our sex lives. It was not a revolution in the conventional sense. It was, in fact, a gadget revolution. And it was one of the most important things that ever happened in this country.

Fads of the Fifties

The affluent fifties did not pass without their fair share of fads and as always the one who paid was the consumer. Kids pestered their parents for Davy Crockett hats and budgies, fun-lovers bought outboard motors and paint-by-number sets and shoppers experienced the ease of drive-in banks and stores.

In 1958 the Hula-Hoop set Canada spinning.

Reducing salons massaged away extra pounds.

Thousands jammed arenas for Monster Bingo where prizes ranged from pop-up toasters to new cars.

A giant milk container was a vending machine.

V-8, Two-Tone, Chrome and Fins

As cars grew longer, lower and wider, you could tell the make, the model and the year a block away. Autumn unveilings were the highlight of the car-buyer's year.

Enormous V-8 engines, two-tone colours, power steering, strips of chrome and stiletto fins became standard on cars that offered "living-room comfort" to eager buyers.

This, we believe, is the finest automobile ever offered
to the luxury-car market

Unlimited chrome—the 1958 Buick Limited.

Ford's popular little T-Bird for 1956.

The look of elegance, with fins of course.

Monarch's Lucerne *with Sun Valley roof.*

The "ivy league" cap was de rigueur.

Looking like the legendary "Bat-mobile," the 1959 Chevy broke all design rules.

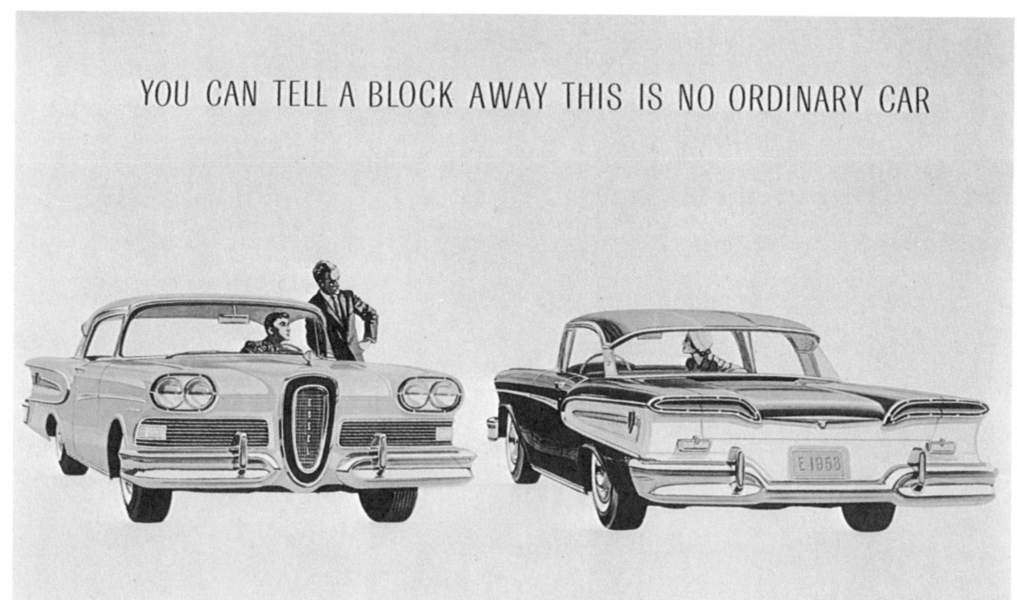

YOU CAN TELL A BLOCK AWAY THIS IS NO ORDINARY CAR
E 1958

Ford's costliest mistake of the '50s, the Edsel sported an ox-yoke front grill (left) and automatic on-the-wheel push-button driving (above).

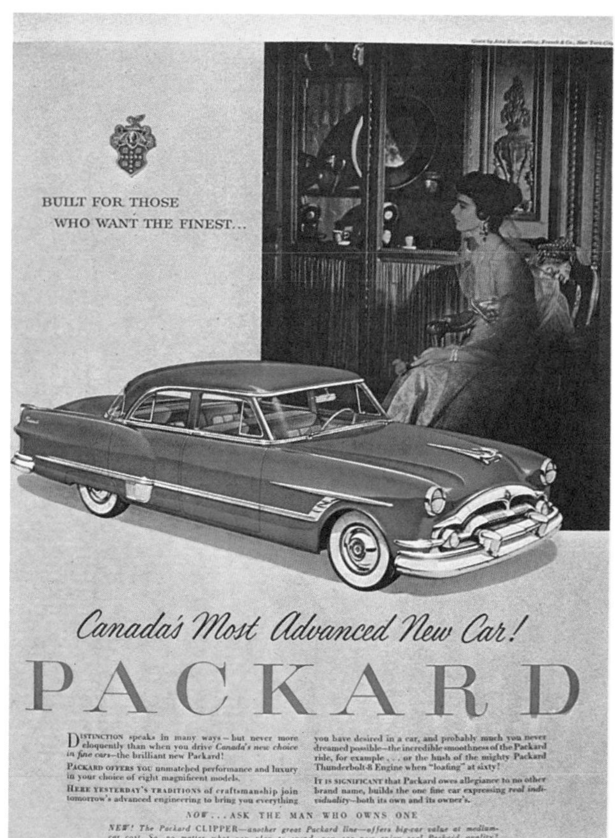

Packard's classic elegance, now a memory.

The Aero Willys—a low-priced alternative.

The built-in Supercharger, standard on Studebaker's Golden Hawk, is typical of Studebaker advances that bring you a better-performing, more economical car. The supercharger delivers extra fuel to the engine only when you need it, while in normal driving you enjoy all the economical benefits of a relatively light engine. It's another Studebaker "first" that makes sense—like Twin-Traction Control, available on all V8's, Luxury-Level Ride, and the new styling—all part of the Craftsmanship that makes the big difference in '57!
Studebaker-Packard
OF CANADA, LIMITED, HAMILTON, ONTARIO
Where pride of Workmanship comes first!

A car-buyer's dream, the Golden Hawk.

STAMPEDE CORRAL

SATURDAY MAY 10

2:30 and 8:30 P.M.

Tickets: HEINTZMANS $2.00 $3.00 $3.50

CHAPTER THREE

The Discovery of the Teenager

The boys sport leather jackets and levis,
but that's their underwear;
the car is their real clothing:

"Saturday Night," Alden Nowlan

When Marilyn Bell scrambled into the black, chilling waters of Lake Ontario late one September night in 1954, she was a perfectly unremarkable sixteen-year-old Canadian girl: a few freckles, a nice grin, a bit pudgy, a little too young to be serious about boys. Nearly twenty-one hours later when she was hauled from the water on the other side of the same lake, limp and semi-conscious, she was the most widely-acclaimed Canadian of her decade – a heroine whose overnight achievement in swimming forty-two miles across Lake Ontario thrilled a generation.

Marilyn was the subject of an almost unexampled orgy of publicity, but newsprint alone could not have transformed this Toronto high-school girl into a celebrity who for years afterward was instantly identifiable as "Canada's sweetheart." What genuinely endeared her to a nation that is notoriously resistant to hero-worship were the virtues that decent people unfailingly admire: courage, endurance against impossible odds, modesty, cheerfulness. She was an ordinary person who unexpectedly achieved something great.

Marilyn was one of the most loudly-acclaimed Canadians of the decade. Another was a restless, olive-skinned boy from Ottawa named Paul Anka who, in April of 1957, dropped out of his grade-ten class and, with the invincible cocksureness of his fifteen years, headed for New York's Tin Pan Alley because, as he explained, "I figured I'd make it faster in the States."

The following year, after selling six million copies of "Diana," a song he had written about his babysitter, Anka had an annual income of $600,000 and was making personal appearances on five continents. His international appeal was astonishing. When he sang in Tokyo, several thousand teenagers huddled in the streets outside his hotel at the height of a typhoon. When he emerged from the hotel, they ripped the sleeve off his shirt. They mobbed his car in the ticker-tape parade and sent him crates of gifts. The Japanese press referred to him as "King Paul."

At a time when Canadian devotion to the British monarchy was waning, our new monarchs were teenagers like King Paul. It was appropriate, for the fifties was the decade when Canada discovered youth.

There had always been a generation gap, of course. From raccoon coats to the 1940s crooners, teenagers had always adopted fads and fashions that were uniquely their own and uniquely distasteful to their elders. In the fifties however, an entire society, suddenly rich in leisure, began to pattern its life-styles after the most leisured seg-

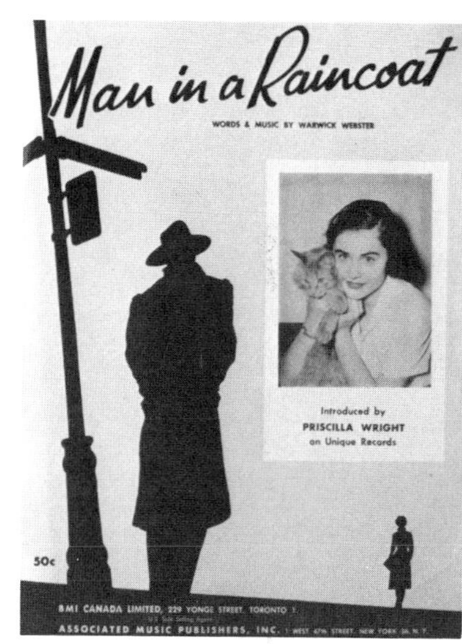

The unexpected million seller of '55 was "Man in a Raincoat" recorded by Priscilla Wright of London, Ontario, thirteen-year-old grand-daughter of Arthur Meighen.

Opposite page: *Calgary promoters corralled thousands of teenagers for this super rock 'n' roll extravaganza.*

The last number of the evening was always a moody ballad danced with your "steady."

ment of the population, the teenagers. A society that began the decade by deploring their ways ended it by imitating them.

There was plenty to deplore in the early fifties. A large and alarmingly visible minority of Canadian teenagers, for instance, affected a tribal costume that could be described as the Hoodlum Look, although nobody called it that. It had been around since the war years. It started with zoot suits and, during the postwar 1940s, had been refined by highly-publicized teenage gangs like Vancouver's Alma Dukes, Winnipeg's Dew Droppers and Toronto's Beanery Boys. By the 1950s there were two essential ingredients: trousers that were baggy at the knee and narrow at the ankle, usually called "strides" or "drapes," and something known as the ducktail haircut, which was short on top and long and greasy on the sides.

strides and hi-tops

Strides were usually custom made of corduroy, black denim or glen plaid. They ranged from a conservative twenty-four inches at the knee and eighteen inches at the ankle to astonishing garments forty-four inches wide at the knee that actually flapped in the breeze like a loose spinnaker. Since strides were seldom mass produced, there was a high degree of individual variation. Some were so narrow at the ankle that you had to open a zipper to get them over your feet. Other models, called "hi-tops," featured a band of material, sometimes decorated with mother-of-pearl buttons, that extended from the waistline up to the navel, or even higher. Girls wore strides too, although seldom of such extreme dimensions.

Ducktail haircuts, also known as boogie cuts, had less variation. You simply told the barber to give you a crewcut on top (he would usually massage your scalp with a hunk of alum to make the hair stand up straight) and leave it long on the sides. You then combed this side-hair straight back until the panels from either side met at the back of your head, literally like a duck's folded-back wings enclosing his back end. There was a female variation of the ducktail haircut known as the Murphy Shag.

The stride-and-ducktail people were a minority. The tribal markings of the less extreme teenagers, however, were just as distinctive. For boys, V-necked sweaters, usually with a white T-shirt showing underneath, were standard. Girls wore sweaters, white blouses, straight or pleated skirts and, invariably, white bobby socks. That was the basic uniform.

pony-tails and pierced ears

Throughout the decade, there were hundreds of minor variations, from year to year and from region to region. For a while, teenage girls scrounged the little purple woollen sacks that originally contained Seagram's Crown Royal rye, and used them as handbags. For anyone of either sex who wore loafers, it was mandatory to stick pennies or nickels inside the instep of each shoe. Cashmere sweaters, worn by either sex, meant status. Brown and white saddle shoes, popularized during the 1940s and earlier, survived into the mid-1950s, then virtually disappeared. Knee-length stockings for girls did not become popular until 1956. Pony-tail hairdos were standard for teenaged girls late in the decade. Pierced ears were popular, but faintly daring. Around 1950, bleached hair for boys enjoyed a brief vogue. Girls used a variation that involved bleaching a wavy stripe in their hair.

Adolescent folkways were as distinctive and as incomprehensible to adults as their clothing. Teenage slang, although its importance was overrated by the press, did exist. In Montreal around 1950, when a girl said, "Sasha, sasha," it meant: "There

45 ROCK 'N' ROLL 45s

Do you remember these hits?

Tutti Frutti
Little Richard
Rock Around The Clock
Bill Haley and the Comets
Blue Suede Shoes
Carl Perkins
Hound Dog
Elvis Presley
The Great Pretender
The Platters
Why Do Fools Fall in Love
Frankie Lymon and the Teenagers
Silhouettes
The Rays
Come Go With Me
The Del Vikings
Bye, Bye Love
The Everly Brothers
Diana
Paul Anka
Get A Job
The Silhouettes
That'll Be The Day
Buddy Holly and the Crickets
Little Darlin'
The Diamonds
School Day
Chuck Berry
Whole Lot-ta Shakin' Goin' On
Jerry Lee Lewis
Young Love
Sonny James
Be-Bop-A-Lula
Gene Vincent
I'm In Love Again
Fats Domino
Singin' The Blues
Guy Mitchell
Party Doll
Buddy Knox
Love Letters In The Sand
Pat Boone
The Twelfth Of Never
Johnny Mathis
The Green Door
Jim Lowe
Honeycomb
Jimmy Rodgers
My Special Angel
Bobby Helms
Poor Little Fool
Ricky Nelson
At The Hop
Danny and the Juniors
Yakety Yak
The Coasters
You Send Me
Sam Cooke
Chantilly Lace
The Big Bopper
Donna
Ritchie Valens
The Book Of Love
The Monotones
To Know Him Is To Love Him
Teddy Bears
My True Love
Jack Scott
Splish Splash
Bobby Darin
Tequila
The Champs
The Purple People Eater
Sheb Wooley
Lipstick On Your Collar
Connie Francis
Teen Angel
Mark Dinning
Kookie, Kookie, Lend Me Your Comb
Ed "Kookie" Byrnes
Teenager In Love
Dion and the Belmonts
Come Softly To Me
The Fleetwoods
Personality
Lloyd Price
Turn Me Loose
Fabian
Mary Lou
Ronnie Hawkins

The Diamonds

From the basement of the Church of St. Thomas Aquinas in Toronto in 1953 to the top of the hit parade with "Little Darlin' " in 1957 was a long haul for this group of Scarborough, Ontario, singers. In 1957 "The Stroll," their second smash hit, had teenagers across the continent doing the new dance step. Like most '50s groups, the four original Diamonds went their separate ways, but their million-selling hits will go down in rock history as classics of the decade.

goes a dreamy-looking guy." In the Ottawa Valley, "lumberjack" was the word for a boy who was not a sharp dresser. "Ishka-lashka bo," in some parts of the country, meant "This is a bad scene; let's get out of here."

Modes of dancing were decidedly pre-electronic. Foxtrots were not scorned at dances in the high-school gymnasium, but "jiving," an arms-length variation of 1940s jitterbugging, was more popular. Pop music was also pretty tame in the early 1950s. The main requirements for a hit, it seems, were mindless lyrics and a catchy tune. One of the decade's biggest hits was recorded in 1954 by four young graduates of St. Michael's Choir School in Toronto. They called themselves The Crewcuts, and the most memorable line of their biggest hit was:

Sh-boom, sh-boom
Ya-ya-ya – ya-ya-ya-yaya
Ya-ya-ya-ya-ya-ya-ya

It sold more than a million copies.

freedom and authority

On the basis of their lyrics, one could conclude that teenagers were pretty removed from social issues. Generally it was a silent, smug, apathetic and altogether unadventurous generation. Dr. Claude Bissell, then president of Ottawa's Carleton University, put it well: "I'm worried that not a single Ottawa resident has written me complaining of the activities of my students. Maturity is all right, but what I fear is premature senility."

Adolescents seemed to carry conformity to truly extravagant lengths during the decade. In 1959, *Maclean's* commissioned a national survey of attitudes toward freedom and authority among high-school students. While not necessarily definitive, the results were disquieting enough to make some educators wonder if the nation was headed for a totalitarian takeover. Ninety per cent of the sample, for instance, agreed with the statement that "obedience and respect for authority are the most important virtues young people should learn." About half the teenagers were in favour of the West launching a preventative war against Russia; "If you don't get them," one boy explained, "they'll get you. So why wait?" About the same proportion were in favour of policemen using third-degree methods to extract confessions, and 60 per cent approved of police wiretapping as a means of gathering evidence.

"It hurts to be left out"

The worst fate imaginable, the survey indicated, was to be an "oddball," an all-purpose word teenagers used to describe anyone who seemed even slightly different. Pressed for a definition, students described oddballs as "lonely people, hoods and queer thinkers," or "a girl who wins all the medals for top marks." A 17-year-old from Winnipeg summed the whole thing up rather well: "The group pretty well runs the show," she said, "and if you don't go along with it you're left out of things. It hurts to be left out. You need the feeling of belonging to people."

The best way of belonging, for many teenagers, was the new ritual of going steady. If you had a steady, nearly all the group activities of teenage life, from dances to beach parties to basketball games, were less perilous. This was even more important than the partner involved. One survey by *Canadian High News* claimed that nearly half the teenagers who had steadies did not really like them much. The essential thing, once again, was to conform, to avoid being an oddball. "There are no mavericks left," commented a psychologist at the Forest Hill Board of Education in Toronto in 1959. "Everybody wants to be like everybody else."

As a group, teenagers were obedient consum-

SASHA-SASHA (Teen Lingo)

Marilyn Bell, Paul Anka, Pat Boone, Annette Funicello and Marlene Stewart were the idols of millions of teenagers in the fifties. But others copied the rougher, tougher, more independent stars like Marlon Brando, James Dean or Sal Mineo. After-school hours or weekends were spent either listening to the latest LP on someone's scratchy little record player (left) or driving to Grand Bend or Wasaga Beach (right) looking for kicks or trouble.

Summer Camp

For half a million Canadian kids, going to camp was an annual pilgrimage that started the day after school ended. It could mean anything from six weeks of swimming, hiking, flickering campfires and toasting marshmallows to an eternity of damp sleeping bags, cranky counsellors, mosquitoes and gnawing homesickness.

Two Pioneer Ranch Camp counsellors wash up at 7:00 AM at Crimson Lake, Alberta.

Five cabin-mates pose for a click of the Brownie Hawkeye at Camp Gay Venture, 1956.

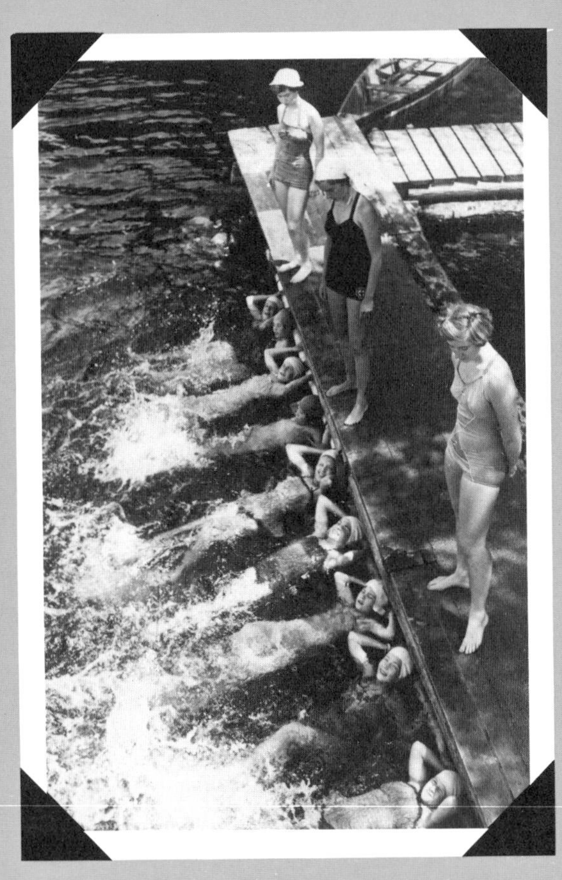

Beginners on the "buddy system" worked all summer for a senior swimmer's badge.

Two uniformed counsellors and their charges crowd the steps of their cabin for a final group picture before returning to textbooks, classrooms and the city's autumn leaves.

ers. Their purchasing power in Canada was worth an estimated $100 million annually. With this kind of money available, and with television functioning as the most potent mass-marketing weapon ever devised, it was inevitable that styles designed for the young would begin to find acceptance among other age groups. At the very least, it meant that fads which had once happened almost accidently now became carefully manipulated events, and that they received more public attention than ever before. Suddenly, it was great to be young.

Even the hula hoop, a juvenile fad if there ever was one, attracted a certain amount of adult interest. It was almost a physiological fact that only the very young were supple enough to keep the hoops twirling around their waists for long periods. One of the more impressive local records was set in 1958 by ten-year-old Pamela Brown of Brantford, Ontario, who twirled a hoop for three hours and five minutes, an estimated 15,938 twirls. But that did not prevent thousands of adults from buying hoops for their own frivolous use. For a while, in fact, hula-hooping became a common after-the-fourth-drink activity at many suburban parties. By the middle of the decade, the spectacle of adults imitating teenage styles was no longer remarkable.

Elvis Presley

Nevertheless, the Davy Crockett fad of 1955 was deplored on the floor of the House of Commons and at the annual convention of the Canadian Humanities Association. But everybody agreed the most alarming phenomenon of all was an ex-truckdriver named Elvis Presley, a rockabilly blues-shouter who wore sideburns, sequined suits and a perpetual sneer, and whose flagrantly sexual stage mannerisms dismayed a generation of parents almost without exception. From the tip of his ducktail to the soles of his blue suede shoes, Elvis Presley was an affront to every value the middle class held dear. When his first film, *Love Me Tender,* opened in Toronto in 1956, it provoked the wildest mob scene in that city's phlegmatic theatrical history. The kids started lining up before dawn and shortly before show time battered down the theatre's doors, bowled over a policeman and two ushers, broke two mirrors, tore down Elvis posters from the walls and used lipstick to scribble "I Love You" on his publicity stills.

The Wild One

The emergence of rock 'n' roll foreshadowed a major shift in popular attitudes. The beatification of Presley and Bill Haley and the Comets (whose Toronto concert appearance caused a near-riot) represented a new style of youthful dissent. Since 1945, the continent had been managed as though it were a moldering family corporation by daddy-figures like St. Laurent and Eisenhower. The generation that reached maturity in the 1950s was heartily sick of them. The kids wanted freedom, chaos, new scenes, excitement, liberation. And they managed to find it in a series of charismatic public figures who ranged all the way from Elvis Presley to, strangely enough, John Diefenbaker.

The James Dean cult was part of the new style; and Marlon Brando's motorcycle movie, *The Wild One;* and progressive jazz, until it was cursed by respectability when Dave Brubeck made the cover of *Time* magazine; and the beat generation.

The beat style started in San Francisco and quickly spawned undergrounds in Vancouver, Toronto and Montreal. Mostly the beats hung around a series of coffee-houses that alternated between cool jazz and folk-singing. They were all very earnest places. At Vancouver's Musicians' and Artists' Club (also known as The Cellar) you could sometimes find Kenneth Patchen, one of San Francisco's beat gurus, reading his poetry to the

On stage at Maple Leaf Gardens in his $10,000 gold lamé suit, the bumping and grinding "pelvis" turned the capacity audience of 18,000 young girls into a shrieking and swooning mob. To them Elvis was the king of rock 'n' roll.

accompaniment of some local jazz ensemble. At Toronto's First Floor Club, where each table was supplied with a candle but custom forebade you to light it, you could hear the folk-singing team of Ian Tyson and Sylvia Fricker performing for the fun of it. And in Montreal in 1958, novelist Hugh MacLennan heard a young poet named Leonard Cohen at a coffee-house called Dunn's and deemed his work sufficiently remarkable to mention it in a magazine piece.

Naturally, beat folkways gradually filtered upward into general use. Hipster slang (dig, crazy, bad scene, cool, groovy, nowhere and something else) could be found a decade later in advertising copy and suburban conversations. Beatnik girls were the first to renounce lipstick and to wear black stockings, straight hair, and coloured eye-shadow – styles that would become popular in the following decade. The coffee-houses would switch from jazz to rock, or become discotheques.

As the decade ended, the beat movement died a natural and honourable death. As a cultural movement, it left few artifacts of lasting value, but it was a precursor of the attitudes that were to characterize the next decade. Despite the "silent generation" label, young people in the fifties turned out to be a force for innovation and change. In any decade, that is what young people are for.

Marilyn Bell

The biggest news story of 1954 was seventeen-year-old Marilyn Bell's forty-mile swim to glory across the cold, choppy waters of Lake Ontario. When she touched shore at the CNE on Sept. 9, she became an instant legend in Canadian sports history, and she received hundreds of gifts, from a pale blue Austin to a year's supply of Wheaties. She conquered the English Channel in '55 and the Strait of Juan de Fuca in '56.

Strapless evening gowns and corsages, rented tuxes and the car for a night – that's what the prom meant in the fifties.

The world's FIRST FEATURE LENGTH
motion picture in
NATURAL VISION
3 DIMENSION

A LION
in your lap!

Arch
Oboler's

A LOVER
in
your arms!

BWANA
DEVIL

in THRILLING COLOR
starring ROBERT STACK · BARBARA BRITTON · NIGEL BRUCE
Released thru
UNITED
ARTISTS

3-D

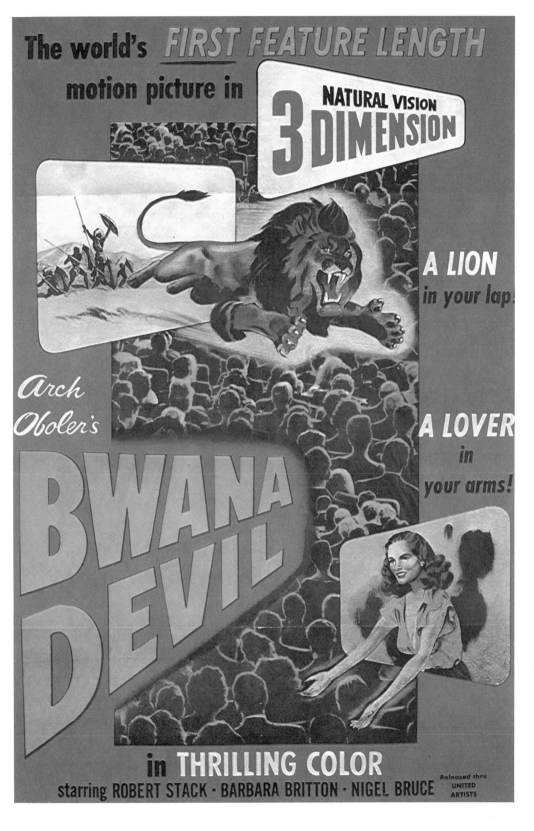

The idea itself wasn't novel – remember the old 19th century stereoscope? – but 3-D (or "the depthies" as they were called) was a valiant attempt by fifties' Hollywood moguls to woo back the tens of millions who had been converted to television. The viewers watched the film through a tinted pair of cardboard and celluloid glasses – one eye saw the images in red, the other in green. The experience was billed "more sensational than real life."

Bwana Devil *was the first 3-D movie to hit the theatres and grossed $95,000 at the box office in its first week.* Maclean's *movie critic, Clyde Gilmour (above), never to be distracted by a fad, commented: "If I had to stay away from one movie for the rest of my life it would have to be* Bwana Devil.*" Gilmour cited the lions for the worst performance by animals in 1953.*

"I'm So Young...

More than anything else, music defined the differences between young and old in the fifties. Only "squares" and parents listened to Patti Page's "Tennessee Waltz," Eddie Fisher's "Oh My Papa," Jo Stafford's "Shrimp Boats" and Frank Sinatra's "Young At Heart." Anyone who was "cool" jived with Elvis Presley, Chuck Berry, The Big Bopper or Jerry Lee Lewis. Teenagers across the country flocked to

record stores with their allowance or earnings to buy the latest "45" or newly-cut Hi-Fi LP. And promoters watched to see which releases were capable of making the Top Ten. Canadians Paul Anka, Jack Scott, the Beau-Marks, the Four Lads, the Crewcuts and the Diamonds all watched at least one of their hit singles climb the charts and turn to gold. Not until the '60s would home-grown talent come into its own.

...and You're So Old"

CHAPTER FOUR

The Entertaining Tyrant of TV

Yes, there it was in front of me: the little square box . . . that was going to ruin my life.

"I Was a TV Addict," Wayne & Shuster

When it finally happened, on September 8, 1952, it didn't really look like the dawn of a new age. First came the test pattern, a busy geometric arrangement of lines and squares, enlivened by a drawing of an Indian, presumably Canadian, wearing a feathered head-dress. (There is some debate on the point, but the consensus among media historians is that it was broadcast upside-down.) Next came an urgent bulletin – two men had robbed a bank and pictures of the suspects were flashed on the flickering blue screen. A puppet show called "Uncle Chichimus" followed.

Finally came the historic moment when the first moving, talking, human Canadian face stepped in front of the big blue camera in the Canadian Broadcasting Company's makeshift Toronto studio, gazed into the voracious eye that would carry his image into ten thousand living rooms, waited until the little red light atop the camera blinked on and began to speak. It was the official beginning of television broadcasting in Canada, and there, in glorious black and white, was Percy Saltzman talking about the weather.

No one could have predicted that Canada's brave new electronic age would be inaugurated by a discussion of the weather, but then, nearly every prediction made about television in the fifties turned out to be sensationally wrong. In an editorial that turned out to be less than prescient, the editor of *Canadian Film Weekly* described TV as a "passing blight." Within three years of this prediction, some two hundred Canadian movie houses had closed their doors. The most spectacularly inaccurate forecast was probably the one delivered by Dr. J.J. McCann, the federal revenue minister whose department was responsible for the Canadian Broadcasting Corporation. "There will be no federal treasury handouts for CBC television," he announced. "The service will pay its own way."

It is plain that television has made children vastly better informed and more sophisticated than children of pre-electronic generations. In the beginning, however, there were plenty of worriers. In a report on the new viewing patterns, one teachers' organization in Toronto fretted: "Surely crouching in a chair or stretching out on the floor for hours in a stuffy, overheated living room cannot be good for any child. What effect will it have on their posture and eyesight?"

Television confounded the prophets by catching on faster than anyone had imagined. Less than two years after the service was introduced, someone bought Canada's millionth set. Since the late 1940s, of course, tens of thousands of Canadians

Johnny Wayne and Frank Shuster were star radio comedians when TV made its appearance in 1952. They conquered the new medium with zany skits that will survive a century.

Opposite page: *When Johnny and Frank laid their cards on a Monte Carlo table, the Riviera was not safe.*

Marshall McLuhan

When Edmonton-born English professor Marshall McLuhan turned his attention to mass communications in 1951, his statements about "hot" and "cool" media and what effects they had on print-oriented society were largely ignored. In the 1960s, with the publication of *Understanding Media*, he was invited into the board rooms of North America to explain this new social order that television and electronic gadgets were creating.

living close to the border had acquired the habit of watching programmes from American stations. "Uncle Milty"–TV comedian Milton Berle–was a household word before the CBC broadcast its first test pattern, and tens of thousands of Canadian children were already familiar with American television characters like Kukla, Fran and Ollie. It wasn't until around the time that millionth set was installed in someone's living room, however, that Canadians began to realize how great was the new medium's impact on their lives.

the voice had pictures

At first, we thought of television simply as an improved form of radio: the voices had pictures connected to them, and wasn't that wonderful. But once you brought a set into your home, it was only a matter of days before you discovered that television was a tyrant as well as an entertainer. The first problem was staying away from it. Owners of new sets would watch anything that flickered, even the stomach-remedy ads and Gorgeous George the wrestler. The second problem was guests who did not own a set. They had a tendency to drop in after supper, when they would be motioned silently to a seat in front of the set, a social ritual that the pre-electronic mind viewed with deep alarm.

The third problem was children. Old Tom Mix westerns, puppet shows and Mickey Mouse cartoons were staple items in the medium's early days. Regulating children's viewing habits thus became an urgent topic at thousands of dinner tables and hundreds of PTA meetings. Homework suffered. The Toronto Women Teachers' Association discovered, to its horror, that children in television homes were spending from twenty-five to thirty hours a week in front of their sets – the equivalent of a double-feature movie every night.

The tenor of family living was altered to an extent that no one could have imagined. It started with rearranging the living-room furniture around the new set. The revolution deepened when the family bought a set of "TV-tables" so they could eat without interrupting their viewing. It gained strength when father began skipping his Wednesday night bowling in favour of an evening in front of the set. The revolution was probably complete when, at eight o'clock on Sunday evenings, a continent that formerly had occupied itself in such diverse pursuits as praying, radio-listening, strolling after supper, lawnmowing, playing Monopoly and even reading, found itself united in watching the "Ed Sullivan Show."

Upper-income families at first disdained television ("I wouldn't have one in the house."); then patronized it ("We've got one, but we only watch 'Omnibus' and the news.") For lower-income families, however, television was not simply a gadget; it was an opiate and a window to the world.

Nobody was prepared for this revolution. A few months before Canadian television went on the air, a committee of advertising men counselled caution: "It would seem rather hazardous for any national advertiser to rob other media to pay for TV."

national television service

The CBC itself, under A. Davidson Dunton, entered the new age with surprising diffidence, and with many false starts. The first application for a private television station in Canada had been made in 1938, but it wasn't until 1948 that the CBC asked the government for the funds it needed to get started. In 1949, the government told the CBC to proceed with stations in Toronto and Montreal. Before they opened, however, the Massey Commission on the Arts, Letters and Sciences urged that no private licences be issued until the CBC was providing a national television service. The government at first agreed, then backed down under pressure from private broadcasters; private licences would be issued, but only in areas not served by the CBC.

The Toronto and Montreal stations opened in 1952; Ottawa and Vancouver the following year. In 1954, Montreal got its second station – the English-language station was the first to open – and Winnipeg and Halifax were added to the chain. By this time, fifteen private stations had also been allowed to open, all of them required to carry at least ten and one-half hours weekly of CBC programmes.

"a brave new world"

At first, these programmes were put together by a small, fanatically dedicated group of young producers who sometimes slept in their offices, worked seven days a week and, more than once in those early months, collapsed from overwork. At one point, the CBC is reported to have considered hiring no producer over thirty, on the grounds that anyone older could not stand the pace. "We all had a feeling of tremendous exhilaration," one alumnus of that period, Harry Rasky, recalled. "Everybody was in love with everybody else's work, and we all believed we were creating a brave new world. We were all novices, and we were all foolishly ambitious. I can't recall a time when the medium was more exciting or more interesting."

After several years of deploring the standards of American television, many Canadian intellectuals were expecting something a great deal worthier from the CBC. To some extent, they got it: Shakespeare; panel shows that brought together several academics to debate the future of Canadian literature; a weekly, half-hour package of intellectual controversy called "Fighting Words"; an earnest and informative series on science; and "Songs from Everywhere," a folk-singing show

Camera 3 moves in for a close-up of Lorne Greene in the TV production of Stratford's Othello. *Hundreds of technicians worked in a maze of lights and cameras to bring Shakespeare to the tube.*

The Shows We Watched

The faces on the following three pages transported Canadians beyond whipping prairie blizzards and cold Maritime nights throughout the golden age of television's first ten years. The CBC embarked on comedy, drama and adventure with shows like "Tugboat Annie," filmed on the Toronto waterfront, "Flight Into Danger" and "Cannonball," but the highlight of CBC programming was the musical variety show which featured talent like Juliette, Bob Goulet, Wally Koster and Shirley Harmer. Although the CBC drew new talent from across the country, many of the performers came to the network from successful careers in radio. Sportscaster Foster Hewitt was one who made the transition from words to words-with-pictures.

Percy Saltzman forecasts cross-country weather.

Foster Hewitt was "Hockey Night in Canada."

Islanders Marg Osborne and Charlie Chamberlain.

"Country Hoedown" featured lanky Tommy Hunter.

"Front Page Challenge" was the top quiz show.

Mike Malone and Jerry Austin of "Cannonball."

Ed McCurdy sang for children on "Ed's Place."

Befreckled Maggie Muggins and Mr. McGarrity.

Jack Kane played saxophone and conducted.

Buxom Jayne Mansfield guested on "Tabloid."

The "Lord of the Wilderness," Pierre Radisson.

Maman Plouffe kept errant offspring in check.

Arthur Hailey wrote "Flight Into Danger."

"Our Pet" Juliette sang with Billy O'Connor.

Wally Koster and Joyce Hahn on "Hit Parade."

Handy Peter Whittall was "Mr. Fix-it."

"The Kindly Landlady," CBC's first melodrama.

Canada's first TV series was "Uncle Chichimus."

"Holiday Ranch" featured fiddler King Ganam.

Bob Goulet and Joyce Sullivan did "Showtime."

Joan Fairfax harmonized with Denny Vaughan.

Tugboat Annie and Shiftless, the first mate.

Nathan Cohen, irascible host of "Fighting Words."

Barry Morse in the drama "Fortune My Foe."

starring Ed McCurdy. Most of these shows made little impression on the general public, however, not because they weren't good, but because "culture" was not what most people wanted to see.

What they did want, mainly, was more American programmes. At first these were not available to the new Canadian network. In the hope of making separate deals with individual stations, American producers initially refused to deal with the CBC. Agreement was not reached until the CBC had been on the air for four months. Then, and only then, did the CBC accept the fact that the majority of its most popular shows would be imported productions. These included "Our Miss Brooks," starring Eve Arden, a series about a small-town schoolteacher that was one of TV's first situation comedies; the "Dennis Day Show," an absolutely undistinguished variety series starring Jack Benny's old sidekick; an equally undistinguished comedy series with Jackie Gleason and Milton Berle; and the "Ed Sullivan Show."

"Radisson" and "Davy Crockett"

When the CBC attempted to imitate its American rivals, the results were seldom successful. Perhaps the best example of this was a programme entitled "Radisson," an earnest attempt to duplicate the impact of Davy Crockett. "The series will develop a Canadian style," a CBC official explained to the press in 1956. Some of the ingredients of this new Canadian style looked remarkably like the old American version. Radisson himself was a Canadianized Fess Parker. The promotional tie-ins were also derivative. There were plans for Radisson coonskin hats (which were actually leftover Crockett coonskins with their tails cut off) Radisson buckskin shirts, Radisson toy rifles, Radisson T-shirts, Radisson dolls, Radisson music boxes, and a Radisson Game with tiny canoes for counters. There was also a Radisson theme-song:

Radisson, Radisson,
Canada's courageous pioneer
Radisson, Radisson
Lord of the Wilderness,
the man who knew no fear.

The series began in February 1957, was greeted with a roar of apathy, and was cancelled before it ran the originally scheduled thirty-nine weeks.

Our pet, Juliette

In those areas where the CBC was not trying to imitate, its productions were usually good, and often brilliant. "Newsmagazine," one of the first programmes, maintained a consistently high standard. "Tabloid," produced by Ross McLean, was the first public-affairs show to prove that television was more than simply an improved version of radio. "Hockey Night in Canada," already a national institution on radio, quickly became one on television, and an assortment of music shows produced several new household names: Gisèle MacKenzie, Shirley Harmer and Don Messer.

The most memorable shows from this period were the ones that were least pretentious. The most popular Canadian production for at least four years was a cowboy-music show called "Holiday Ranch." Its star was Cliff McKay, a paunchy clarinet-player who had once been in The Happy Gang; he signed off each show with "Wherever you are, folks, remember, tomorrow is Sunday." Another Saturday-night institution was Juliette Augustina Sysak Cavazzi, better known as "Our pet, Juliette." She came on just after the news and just before the wrestling, her most requested songs were "Shine On Harvest Moon" and "Roses of Picardy," her stage manner was pure treacle and she was so popular that, after she mentioned that she was dieting, so many fans sent in recipes that the CBC had to print a form-letter reply.

NEXT WEEK'S
Highlights
on TV
by GORDON SINCLAIR

Two good Canadian shows are back for another season. Johnny Wayne and Frank Shuster, by far our funniest comedians, on CBLT-CHCH at 8. The Plouffe Family, which drew small ratings in Ontario, but contributed oodles to English-French understanding (and was a warm, homey show in addition) at 10:30.

Saturday

8:30—Seasonal debut of "Holiday Ranch," where host Cliff McKay has run into trouble getting a warbler who can project. The way I get it Cliffo has signed a Montreal chanteuse. This was top Canadian show of last season; looks okay again.

9:00—The first drama of the season's "On Camera" series has a promising theme. The private life of a hangman. They call it "Alias Mr. Pollard" with Irving Lerner as the executioner.

11:10—Billy O'Connor: reliable tries by a singer who can't sing but has fun anyhow.

Sunday

9:30—Shirley Harmer comes back for another season in a song and dance show that seems unchanged from last year. With Don Garrard, choreography by Don Gillies and special dances by Al and Blanche Lund. Orchestra under Howard Cable.

Gordon Sinclair surveyed new CBC offerings for the fall of 1955 in a candid column for the Toronto Star.

Roger Lemelin

Creator of the captivating Plouffe family, Roger Lemelin wrote both the English and French scripts for the weekly show that sewed up TV ratings across the country during the fifties. Born in a working-class district north of Montreal, Lemelin completed his first novel while he was working in a lumber camp in 1944. The best-selling novelist's literary achievements include a Guggenheim Fellowship, a Rockefeller Foundation Scholarship and the prestigious Prix des Lettres et des Arts in Paris, 1954.

Apart from "Hockey Night in Canada" or the annual Grey Cup telecasts, however, the CBC failed to produce a show that united all of English-speaking Canada in a single, collective experience. In Quebec, where competition from American programming scarcely existed, there was nothing to imitate. The result was the emergence of a television style that was bold, original and popular. One of the medium's early heroes in Quebec was René Lévesque, a journalist who became famous throughout the province as a public-affairs host. He was one of the leaders of a strike of television producers in Montreal late in the decade and, from the experience, extracted some of the political insights that later propelled him to a position of leadership in Quebec's quiet revolution.

Lemelin's "Les Plouffe"

The outstanding example of Quebec's television style was Roger Lemelin's incredibly popular dramatic series, "Les Plouffe." It became a weekly ritual throughout Quebec and, to a lesser extent, throughout the rest of the country via a watered-down English version. It was the story of a working-class Quebec family. Papa Théophile was a plumber, and the two older children worked in a shoe factory. One daughter, Cécile, was a spinster who had been engaged for years to a bus driver. One son was a budding athlete, another a dreamy intellectual. Maman, naturally, was the centre of the family, gabby, warm-hearted and continually scheming on behalf of her children.

Like Britain's "Coronation Street" serial, the Plouffe family was almost a televised national anthem, a statement in dramatic terms of everything that French Canada wanted to believe about itself. As such, it became one of the most involving television shows ever produced anywhere. Priests sometimes shortened their services on Wednesday evenings, so that parishioners would not miss the show. Hockey schedules in St. Jerome and Quebec City were altered to avoid Wednesday night games. Theatre attendance throughout the province was down on Wednesday nights and, in Montreal, where four out of five French-speaking television homes were tuned to the show, police thought they detected a lessening in traffic congestion between 8:30 and 9:30 on Wednesday nights. In 1954, a Quebec firm printed a Plouffe jigsaw puzzle and sold 140,000 copies in the three weeks just before Christmas.

The English-language network, meanwhile, concentrated on improving its technical facilities to the point where it would constitute a truly national service. A coast-to-coast microwave link was inaugurated in 1958. At the same time, the installation of six videotape machines in Calgary made it possible, for the first time, for the same programme to be seen in the same time-slot in various time-zones across the country.

In 1957, in a bold attempt to move with the times, the CBC relaxed its commercial acceptance regulations to allow deodorant advertising. But ads for brassieres, girdles, laxatives, funeral homes, kidney regulators and mining stocks remained on the unacceptable list.

hair spray ads and hockey

The content of television – the situation comedies, hair-spray ads and hockey games – was what engaged our attention at the time. But nothing that was broadcast, not even "Les Plouffe," had as great a social impact as the mere fact of television itself. Whether the CBC had broadcast nothing but westerns, or nothing but symphonies, the medium's social effects would have been approximately the same. People would still have watched, and their lives would have been changed regardless of the content.

It was a Canadian who first grasped the importance of this fact and then popularized it with a slogan that was destined to become one of the chief catchwords of the next decade: The medium is the message. Marshall McLuhan was saying it at the University of Toronto as early as the mid-1950s. Together with an anthropologist named Edmund Carpenter, he began exploring the effects of the various media on human sensibility and, in his dazzling, contradictory way, began shooting out pinwheel insights in all directions. Many of them were contained in a remarkable magazine called *Explorations* that he and Carpenter edited.

Most of their observations about the effect of media on our senses were based on brilliant speculative insights. But these were reinforced by occasional experiments that may one day be regarded as extremely important, because they were among the first attempts at formulating a communications theory, a field that can only grow in importance as this century proceeds.

Until McLuhan's ideas became popular, nearly all criticism of television had been made in pre-television terms. To the literate man, that is, the man whose thought-processes had been formulated by print, television was either "highbrow" or "lowbrow," depending on its content. He did not realize, until McLuhan suggested it, that television would make such distinctions practically meaningless.

Of all the revolutions that occurred in the 1950s, television was the most basic. It not only changed our lives, it even changed the way we viewed those changes.

Great Voices of Radio

Television sounded radio's death knell. Listeners became viewers, advertisers switched their dollars to TV, and recorded music replaced live orchestras in radio drama. These nine radio personalities held their own successfully.

Dramatic actor John Drainie

Max "Rawhide" Ferguson

Broadcaster Kate Aitken

Interviewer Elwood Glover

Producer Andrew Allan

Newsman Earl Cameron

Commentator James Minifie

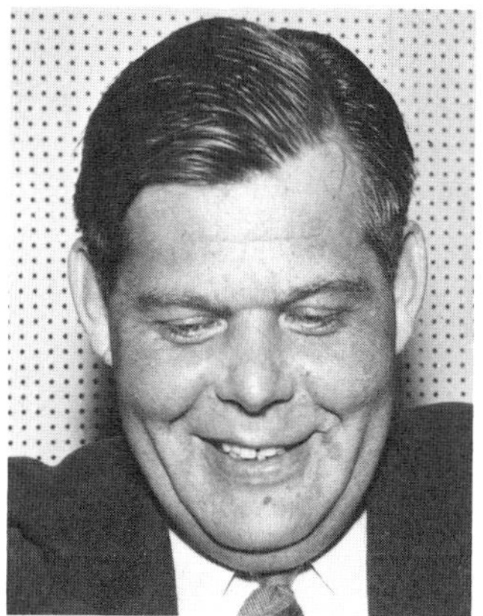

"Small Types" Byng Whitteker

Playwright Lister Sinclair

NOTRE BUT
UN CANADA UNI D'UN OCÉAN À L'AUTRE
CKVL
CRAWLEY FILMS
CFRA
CKCH
CKAC

CHAPTER FIVE

Working for the Yankee Dollar

Instead of being owners ourselves of our resources we will wake up some day to find we are owers . . .

"Mr. Canada," John Fisher, 1950

We knew exactly what an American looked like. He drove a huge, bloated automobile. He wore a Hawaiian shirt, bermuda shorts and a baseball cap. He usually had a cigar clamped in his mouth, but that did not prevent him from talking loudly in restaurants. His wife wore toreador pants and hair curlers; his kids wore faded blue denim and sneakers and had no manners.

It was a crude caricature, but it surfaced everywhere throughout the fifties: in editorial cartoons, in conversations, and occasionally, during the tourist season, on the street. The image symbolized the ambivalence that Canadians felt toward their nearest neighbour. As our ties with Britain loosened, our network of associations with the United States – economic, cultural and military – became more complex and more visible.

Canadians reacted to this new situation with mixed emotions, among which envy and contempt were prominent. We accepted American capital, American technology and American management techniques, and we realized that these things were helping to create our new prosperity. At the same time, we tended to blame the Americans for everything that was new and unwelcome. "All that is loud, noisy and vulgar on our little scene is supposed to be due to American influence," wrote Hugh MacLennan in 1958. "If the manners of our children are bad, if they don't read, pray, think or wash their faces, the Americans are blamed for it."

We deplored their comic books, although our children (and not a few adults) bought them by the millions. We derided their television programmes, but usually watched them in preference to our own. We felt smugly immune to the excesses of McCarthyism, we fondly assumed that our schools were superior to theirs, and we regaled each other in a thousand cocktail-party conversations about their incredible ignorance of Canada, (the usual example being some American tourists who, on their first visit to Toronto or Winnipeg, had demanded to see the igloos. We took a yokelish and faintly malevolent pride in the fact that our dollar was worth more than theirs. Canadians who visited American border cities such as Bellingham or Buffalo would get offended by the bartenders and soda-jerks who had never seen a Canadian dollar and refused to believe it was worth more than the Yankee greenback. We deplored the way they treated their racial minorities and persisted in our smugness even after Farley Mowat reported in *People of the Deer* that some of our own Eskimos were starving.

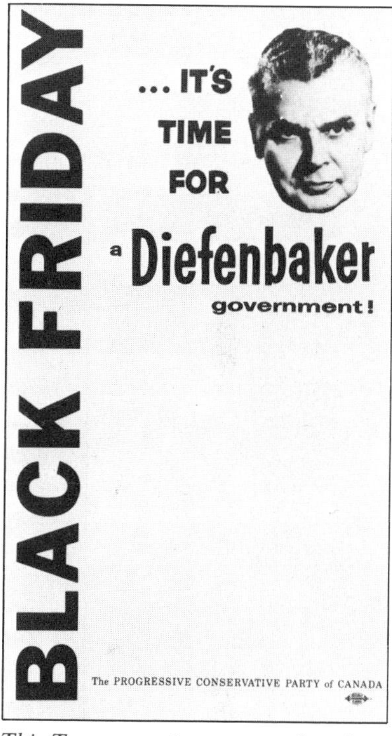

This Tory campaign poster referred to Black Friday, that day in 1956 when the Liberals forced closure on debate over the pipeline issue.

Opposite page: *Two years after his leadership victory in 1956, "Dief the Chief" paraded the Tories to the largest majority ever given a Prime Minister. A traditionally Liberal Quebec contributed massive support.*

Peter C. Newman

Vienna-born immigrant Peter C. Newman launched his career as a journalist during the fifties as News Editor of the *Financial Post* and Ottawa Editor of *Maclean's*. His preoccupation with economic and political power coloured the pages of newspapers and magazines throughout the decade. *Flame of Power* profiled the men who held the balance of economic power in Canada, and the best-selling *Renegade in Power* was a searing view of the Diefenbaker years.

These were not the responses of a confident people. The fact is that, during the 1950s, Canada moved absent-mindedly into a state of economic dependence on the United States that had not been paralleled since the 1920s. This process has often been pictured as a sell-out straight and simple, as though a handful of greedy capitalists had somehow conspired to deliver our resources and our birthright to their Wall Street masters. In fact, it was a lot more complex.

American money

For one thing, Canada needed American investment; it is doubtful that Canadian savings, even assuming they could have been mobilized for the task, would have been sufficient to generate the prosperity that Canadians demanded. For another, our open-arms attitude toward foreign capital was not pursued against the will of the majority of Canadians. A Gallup poll taken in 1951 asked Canadians if they felt there was too much American influence. A little more than one-third of those questioned thought so, and 16 per cent had no opinion; but nearly one-half of those questioned felt that American influence was not excessive.

Among this near-majority was Clarence Decatur Howe, the American-born engineer who had managed Canada's wartime economy and, as Minister of Trade and Commerce and Minister of Defence Production, was indisputably the most powerful man in the country. His word was final on all matters concerning economic policy (members of the CCF party sometimes referred to him as Clarence "Dictator" Howe), and he was emphatically in favour of accepting all the American capital he could attract. In his public statements, one of his favourite themes was to warn against "narrowly nationalistic and emotional attitudes towards foreign capital."

In the earlier part of the decade, he need not have worried. In 1950 alone, American companies invested $167 million in 30 new Canadian subsidiaries, (bringing the total of American-controlled Canadian subsidiaries to 2,200) and another $363 million in Canadian-controlled enterprises. That same year, American investment in Canada totalled nearly $7 billion – which was about one-third of all American investments abroad. What this added up to, in 1950 alone, was an American investment of nearly $40 for every man, woman and child in Canada. Charles Wilson of General Motors, the Detroit tycoon who won immortality of a sort by remarking that "What's good for General Motors is good for the United States," explained why. "This is a vast storehouse of agricultural and mineral wealth waiting for further development," he told a respectful audience of Canadian businessmen. "GM is bullish on Canada."

Canadian businessmen used to enjoy hearing that sort of thing. A concerned minority wondered about the risks involved in harbouring so much outside money, but most Canadians, in that self-satisfied postwar era, felt rather pleased at all the attention from abroad.

vast new deposits

And there is no question that under C.D. Howe's stewardship, Canada in the 1950s became one of the world's most attractive investment areas. The political climate was stable and the returns were good. Even more important, the natural resources were there at a time when alternate sources of supply, for a variety of reasons, were less than certain. The United States needed petroleum; the discovery of Alberta's Leduc field in 1947 provided all the oil they needed. Faced with the imminent prospect of depletion of the Mesabi range, the American steel belt badly needed iron ore; the development of the Ungava iron ore region would supply all the ore that could be used. Sudbury supplied nickel, and when that was not enough, the vast new deposits near Thompson, Manitoba, were developed. Our uranium fuelled the American weapons-development programme.

If it was American capital that paid for most of these developments and collected most of the profits in return, Canadians had no one to blame but themselves. For there is little doubt that, during the 1950s, American investors showed far more faith in Canada than Canadians did. When risk was involved, Canadians were not interested.

pay-off at Leduc

Imperial Oil, for instance, spent $23 million in Alberta drilling 133 dry wells before the gamble paid off with the Leduc strike. As early as 1951, some 500 uranium deposits had been registered through the north; but few Canadians gambled money on exploration until the mid-1950s, after Americans had shown the way. We even shied away from resource developments that were relatively free of risk. Canadian government geologists discovered the Ungava region's vast iron ore deposits in 1895, but it took an American initiative to raise the money to build the railroad to get the ore to market. Even then, Ungava's developers approached Canadian insurance companies first to borrow the necessary funds. These companies advanced only $2 million; the other $143 million had to be borrowed in the United States.

The issue was far from theoretical. In 1958, Ford of Canada refused to consider an order from "Red" China for 1,000 cars and trucks, an order worth between $2 and $3 million dollars, because American law prohibited trade with most Communist countries. Under American law, which extended to Canadian subsidiaries, the sale was illegal; under Canadian law it was not. The fact that a

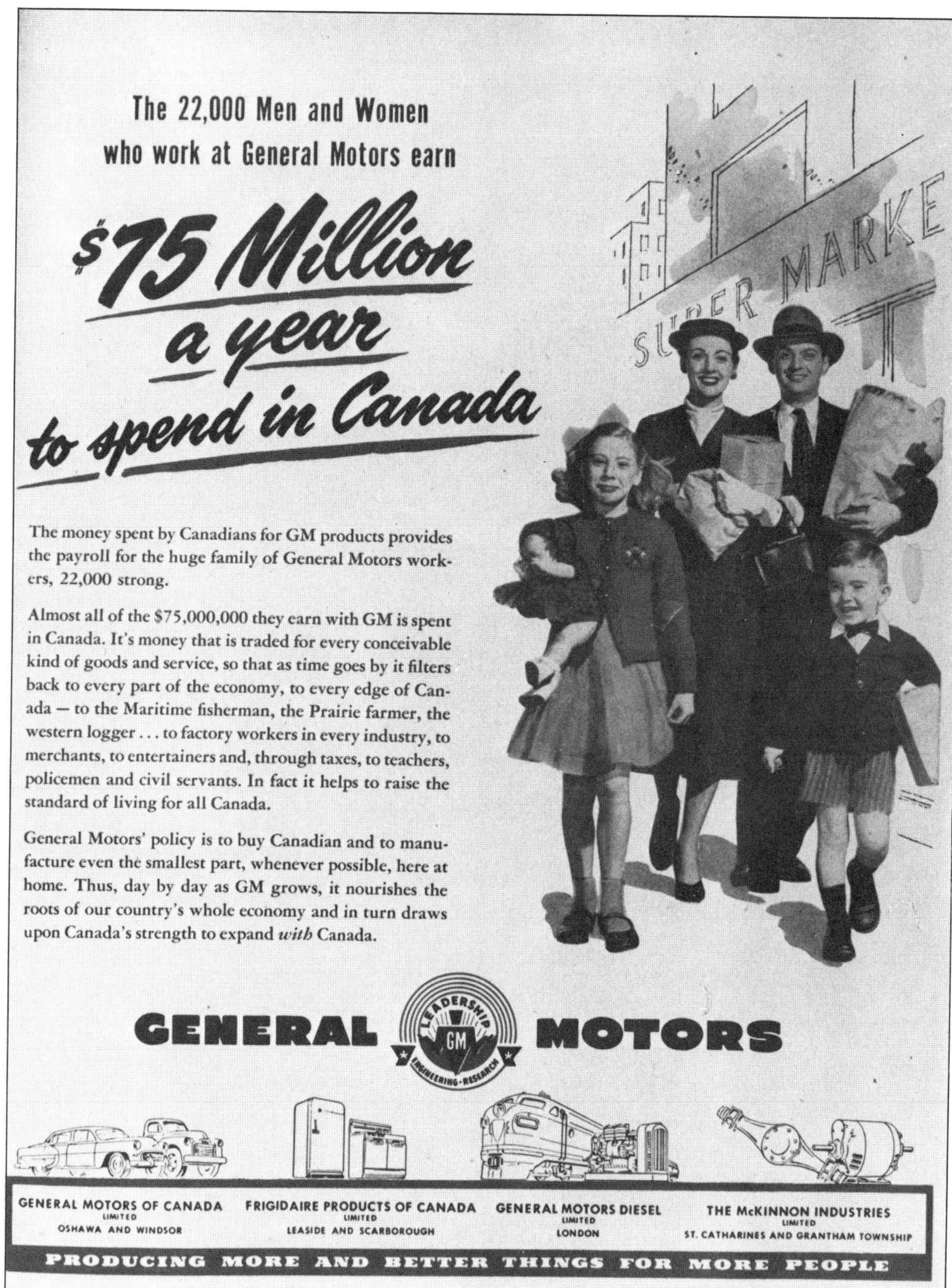

American-owned firms fuelled Canadian prosperity with money and jobs, witness this 1953 ad.

This hydroelectric station being constructed near Cornwall, Ontario, was a link in the mammoth project that strung power lines along the route of the St. Lawrence Seaway.

corporate resident of Canada had no choice but to obey the laws of a foreign country underlined what economic domination meant in everyday terms.

One book about Canadian-American relations, *Good Fences Make Good Neighbors,* supplied another piquant example. It told of a Calgary newspaper editor who had supported Britain's action in the Suez crisis and had written editorials condemning the American position. As a result some American members of Calgary's Ranchmen's Club threatened to blackball the editor if he applied for membership. "Can you imagine the impression this made on Canadian members?" one member asked. "Here was a coterie of Americans who were bent on keeping a Canadian out of a Canadian club because he opposed the foreign policy of the United States." If there were Ugly Americans, however, there were also Ugly Canadians. During the 1956 debate on the pipeline, some American executives in Calgary found the words "Dirty Yank" spelled out on their front lawns in weed-killer, and some of their children were picked on in Calgary public schools.

"a forty-ninth state"

Despite the fact that Canadians declined to put their own dollars into their own resources, however, it came as a shock when we discovered how much corporate control we had given by default to the Americans. In 1956, the Dominion Bureau of Statistics revealed that American firms controlled more than half of Canadian manufacturing – including 90 per cent of the automobile industry, 68 per cent of the oil industry, 41 per cent of the drug industry, and 39 per cent of the pulp and paper industry. Of the 60 companies in Canada with assets of more than $25 million, fewer than half were Canadian-controlled. In Ontario, only 45 of the 115 manufacturing operations established in 1955 were Canadian-owned.

Although the situation was not without precedent (foreign control of Canadian manufacturing had risen above the half point in the 1920s), public reaction to this report was immediate. People protested what appeared to be the slow erosion of our sovereignty, and the Liberal government attracted most of the blame. If the Liberals were re-elected, said John Diefenbaker, Canada would become "a virtual forty-ninth economic state in the American union."

Canada's Economic Prospects

One reflection of this public concern was the report in 1958 of the Royal Commission on Canada's Economic Prospects. It was headed by Walter Gordon, whose name was to become a synonym for economic nationalism. The commission deliberated for several years and its inquiries became, in effect, a massive research project that attempted to answer the question of where Canada was headed, and how we should get there.

Although the Commission emphasized that foreign money should continue to be welcomed in Canada, it proposed a series of safeguards under which that money should be accepted. It urged that foreign-controlled corporations be required to publish financial statements in Canada, include Canadians on their boards of directors, and offer an appreciable amount of their stock to Canadians. The Commission also recommended legislation to ensure that control of banks and insurance and financial companies would remain in Canada.

Ironically, it was Canada's performance in the foreign policy field that did much to counter-balance our concern over the prospect of American domination. Our cars and television programmes may have been American, and most of our industry may have been owned by Americans, but in the area of international diplomacy, Canada steered a course that was firmly resistant to American pressures. It was more than a question of simply daring to disagree occasionally with American Foreign Secretary John Foster Dulles. It involved the development of an entirely new diplomatic style, and a new and important role for Canada in the councils of the world.

Most of the credit, of course, belonged to Lester B. Pearson, then External Affairs Minister. He was both a product and a creator of Canada's distinct diplomatic style: civilized, moderate, scholarly, sophisticated. Through the 1950s, he painstakingly attempted to steer an independent course between British and American policies. He set the tone as early as 1951, when he told a Toronto audience:

The days of relatively easy and automatic political relations with our neighbour are, I think, over. While we are most anxious to work with the United States and support her in the leadership she is giving to the free world, we are not willing to be merely an echo.

In an apparent reference to Washington's pressure for a major Canadian contribution to the Korean war effort, Pearson said:

Americans should not attempt to tell us that until we do one-twelfth or one-sixteenth or some other fraction as much as they are doing in some particular enterprise, we are defaulting. It would also help if the United States took more notice of what we do, and indeed occasionally of what we say. The only time the American people seem to be aware of our existence is when we do something they don't like.

Most Canadians applauded this. And the vigilant *Chicago Tribune* referred to Pearson as a "pinko."

The St. Lawrence Seaway provided one spectacular demonstration of this new-found unwillingness to be an American "echo." The joint project had been under consideration since at least the

Champlain at the Seaway and Radisson at the Pipeline: five hundred years of exploration and progress reflected in these Bank of Nova Scotia advertisements.

When Opportunity
KNOCKS...
HADLEY
COLLEGE
JAMAICA
Canada Savings Bonds
...give You a chance to say "Yes"!

Canadians usually put their money into savings bonds and banks when opportunity knocked in the fifties. By 1955, American firms controlled over half of our capital investment.

Opposite page: *The Toronto Stock Exchange was the busiest "gambling house" in Canada. The floor trader in this photo has just completed a transaction and uses hand signals to inform the brokerage clerks who are seated around the trading floor.*

1920s, but had always floundered on the objections of port and railway lobbyists in the American Congress. In the beleaguered atmosphere of the early 1950s, it was only natural that they should justify their objections on the grounds of national security. The Association of American Railroads warned that the Seaway would be highly vulnerable to enemy air attacks. Around the same time, the mayor of New York, whose city feared a loss of seaport trade if the project went through, called the project visionary, madcap, a gross waste and warned patriotically that its construction would be "a death blow to American world trade prestige."

NATO and NORAD

Finally Ottawa announced that it would go ahead on the Seaway, without help from the United States. Faced with the prospect of being shut out of one of the twentieth century's major developments, and under increasing pressure from steel producers, Congress finally caved in and ratified the joint agreement.

The Liberal government, mostly at Pearson's initiative, came to the centre of the world stage in more direct ways. During the Suez crisis it was Pearson, resisting great pressure at home and abroad, who refused to support the Anglo-French intervention. And it was Pearson again who, in one of the decade's major diplomatic feats, engineered the creation of a United Nations peacekeeping force to separate the warring parties in the canal zone. For this achievement he received the Nobel Peace Prize in 1957. The Liberals also insisted on tough guarantees of our sovereignty when they negotiated the terms of Canada's membership in NATO and the North American Air Defence (NORAD) agreement.

Even C.D. Howe, the minister most frequently accused of selling out to the United States was aware of the paramount importance of safeguarding Canadian interests. Ironically, it was this insistence on protecting our interests in natural gas development that led to the Liberal government's downfall.

There was no question that the easiest way to get Alberta natural gas to markets in the United States and eastern Canada was by building a pipeline through the United States. But Howe insisted on a pipeline that would follow an all-Canadian route. When the American interests that had agreed to build the pipeline experienced difficulty raising the necessary funds, they approached Ottawa for help. Howe agreed to advance Trans-Canada Pipe Lines Ltd. an $80 million loan to complete the Alberta-Winnipeg section of the line, at 5 per cent interest, and with serious penalties in the event of default.

"American pipeline buccaneers"

What happened when Howe laid this deal before Parliament is now history. In order for construction to begin on schedule, he needed parliamentary assent by May 1956. Faced with this inflexible deadline, the government invoked closure in advance of debate, thus revealing what appeared to be an arrogance and contempt for legislative process that, a year later, put the Liberals out of office. The "American pipeline buccaneers" were prominent among the demons that John Diefenbaker invoked against the Liberals in his successful 1957 election campaign. Diefenbaker's electoral vision seemed to promise Canadians a new posture of independence from American influence.

We did not solve the problems posed by American influences on our culture and economy and foreign relations in the 1950s. But at least we saw the problems more clearly than ever before.

39

"The Look" of the Fifties

for women was made up of many components...

(1) See-thru nylon blouses with puffed sleeves; (2) The poodle cut; (3) Scalloped hats with veils; (4) Pop-it beads and full, red lips; (5) Flats, felt skirts and raglan sleeves; (6) Tight sweaters and short shorts with white bucks; (7) Boat necks, pedal pushers and saddle shoes; (8) Home perms; (9) Spike heels and seamed nylons with crinolines; (10) The "sack"; (11) Strapless gowns; (12) The tailored suit; (13) Straight skirts and Queen Anne heels; (14) Tube tops and velvet chokers; (15) One-piece swimsuit with shirred panel; (16) Blue denim and flannel plaid, bobby socks and penny loafers.

12
13
16
10
11
14
15

... to Farm Fields

...inion Tar—

... farm productivity are ... varied activities of ...es.

...ompany supplies, among other ...hat makes possible the removal of ...nd airfields. Canada Creosoting ... fencing of farm fields and pastures, ...arm buildings.

...sidiaries, Dominion Tar & Chemical ...products, providing stability for its ... scope for its employees.

DTC

TAR & CHEMICAL COMPA...

Subsidiaries of Dominion Tar & Chemical Company, Limit...

Canada Roof Products, Limited
Chemical Developments of Canada Limited
... Cooksville Company, Limited
... Corporation Limited
SIPOREX ...

ALL CANADIAN

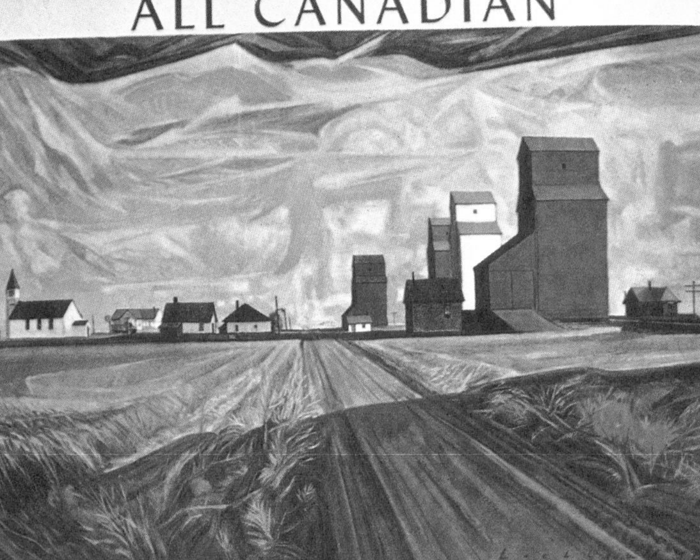

"Prairie Village" was painted by the Canadian artist Kenneth C. Lochhead, S.S.A. This is one of a series of paintings depicting all-Canadian scenes commissioned by Canadian Oil Companies, Limited. With the full co-operation of The National Gallery of Canada, several of this country's most distinguished artists were selected to portray their impressions of their native land. Reproductions of this painting, (18" x 14½") suitable for framing, are available on request at no charge. Request forms may be obtained at all White Rose Dealers.

Nowhere can Canada's prairie provinces be matched for startling contrast. A vast, rolling plateau high in the clouds, its centre an Eden of blazing wildflowers and fruits, surrounded by waving fields of wheat of a quality never matched elsewhere in the world, flanked by the breath-taking Rockies. Home of the scarlet-coated Mounties, the fabulous gold, copper, platinum of Flin-Flon, the booming oil towns.

Broad, delightful highways now invite you, where once the storied Red River carts rumbled. Be ready for an experience in grandeur—grandeur that is all-Canadian.

Canadian Oil Companies, Limited too is *all Canadian*—from the Rockies to the Atlantic wherever you drive, White Rose Dealers are ready to serve you, with top quality petroleum products.

Known from the Rockies to the Atlantic as "The Pick of Them All".

WHITE ROSE · THE PICK OF THEM ALL!

CANADIAN OIL COMPANIES, LIMITED

The All-Canadian Company

Producers, Refiners and Marketers

To produce more food more cheaply

To bring a better standard of living to the world

Two Great World-Wide Organizations Unite

MASSEY M-H HARRIS

AND

Ferguson

Massey-Harris, pioneer in the farm implement industry, pioneer in power-farming equipment and world-leader in the self-propelled combine, now becomes greater than ever by the acquisition of Ferguson—pioneer in the application of hydraulics and the mounting of implements to make tractor and implement an integral unit—known universally as The Ferguson System, which has been much imitated but never duplicated.

...the pooling of engineering skills, the more ... of manufacturing facilities and ... under a single ... Massey-

The Company will continue to market the two lines separately under their well-known trade names: "Massey-Harris" and "Ferguson"

...LIMITED

Footwear for the well-dressed spaceman

Even a spaceman ready to blast off for Mars at any moment, is still an earth-bound little boy in terms of footwear—as any family's shoe bill will show you. Luckily for everyone concerned, synthetic rubber has entered the constant battle between boy and boot, on the side of the boot. It has more than *doubled* shoe sole life.

This boon to spacemen's parents is made possible by one of the twenty-five types of Polysar* rubber being made in the 160 acre plant of the Polymer Corporation in Sarnia. There are, of course, many other kinds of Polysar rubbers. In fact, you would have difficulty in getting along in your everyday life without them. Polysar is constantly adding to the convenience of living, because Polysar is rubber designed to be best for the job.

SYNTHETIC RUBBER

*Registered trade mark

POLYMER CORPORATION LIMITED

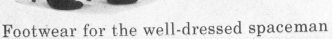

CHAPTER SIX

Opening the Last Frontier

People said the North could wait.
We went ahead.

Gilbert LaBine to Peter C. Newman, 1959

It all began in the summer of 1952 when Gilbert LaBine, one of the fathers of the industry, received a coded telegram from one of his field geologists in northern Saskatchewan. "Come quick," it read, "I've shot an elephant." With this cryptic message, the uranium boom was on.

Gunnar Gold Mines Ltd., which had financed the exploration around Lake Athabaska, jumped from 40 cents to $12 a share. Rival prospectors moved in, set up tents and shacks, and within weeks the area, soon to be designated Uranium City, resembled another Klondike. By the time the Gunnar mine went into production in 1955, Uranium City was an authentic frontier community – transient, colourful, brawling and bizarre.

The Canadian north was our last frontier, one that developed in response to the needs of twentieth-century technology and twentieth-century warfare. It was a frontier that was managed by giant corporations, not by individual adventurers. And because this was the 1950s, not the 1880s, it was a frontier that operated in the hinterland amid the trappings of affluence. Instead of a mule train winding over the Klondike trail, this frontier sported brand new Pontiacs being air-lifted into instant communities.

This northern frontier was the foundation of our affluence; the postwar boom that continued throughout the fifties was based on natural resources. The world, especially the United States, needed Canadian oil, iron, uranium, natural gas and the aluminum that could only be refined with Canadian hydroelectric power. To get these raw materials to the market, we turned dozing hamlets into brawling boomtowns, strung the world's longest pipeline halfway across the country and, in one of the biggest construction jobs in the history of the world, scooped out a gigantic Seaway to connect a string of Great Lakes cities with the Atlantic Ocean.

In terms of economic growth, the boom of the 1950s was not the nation's biggest, but it was one of the most dramatic because it affected so many people – not simply their incomes, but their environments and their imaginations as well. For the first time since the twenties, large numbers of people found themselves earning big money, or believing that they soon would be. Millionaires proliferated, and many of them were flamboyant spenders like Joe Hirshhorn and Frank McMahon who impinged on the national consciousness in a way that the cautious old money of the banks and trust companies never had. They helped disseminate the mystique of glamour, excitement and easy money that pervaded the decade. Capitalism appeared to be delivering the goods at last; and

By the early fifties, long distance connected the corporate executive to the outposts and oil fields and mine shafts of the last frontier.

Opposite page: *These ads from some of Canada's biggest manufacturers attest to affluence in the booming fifties. The last frontier meant many things to different people, but to everyone willing to take a risk, it meant a chance at big money.*

SIX WHO MADE MILLIONS

Multi-Magnate E.P. Taylor

Uranium King Joseph Hirshhorn

Maritime Tycoon K.C. Irving

Meat Packer Fred Mendel

Oil Baron Frank McMahon

News Mogul Roy Thomson

thousands of Canadians learned to regard the economic system as a sort of fairy godmother who could, and often did, touch ordinary people with a golden wand.

In St. Blaise, Quebec, four brothers, all of them hard-working farmers, staked claims in Barraute township in their off-hours and found that some of their ore samples were strong in silver and zinc. They sold their claims for $150,000, donated $425 to the church, bought drinks for everybody in the village and new Pontiac sedans for themselves, then calmly resumed farming. A small Indian band with a reservation near Edmonton received at least $100,000 for mineral rights to their land. When Gunnar Mines made their huge uranium strike in northern Saskatchewan, an unsuccessful prospector named Gus Hawker set up a general store in a tent and accepted mining claims as payment for groceries. Within a matter of months he had acquired six hundred claims and sold two hundred of them for $210,000. All through the 1950s, stories like these were regular newspaper fare. Canada had known prosperity before, but never had so many Canadians believed in so many fairy-tales.

penny stocks

This optimism was reflected most directly in the stock exchanges. Between 1949 and 1951, the value of Canadian industrial stocks more than doubled. Base metal stocks did even better. In one day, May 29, 1950, Calgary's unpretentious stock exchange traded more than one million shares, most of them penny stocks of obscure oil companies. A lot of this activity was solidly grounded in economic realities, but most of it was simply wishful thinking by credulous investors on both sides of the border. Two brokerage houses hired night staffs to keep up with the 1951 trading volume, including the orders of an evangelist from

Los Angeles, who, along with her money, sent a note to her broker: "I pray God," she wrote, "who alone knows just what is under the ground in Alberta, Canada, to touch the hands of the drillers to place the drilling bit at the right place."

The uranium boom was the definitive boom of the fifties. The industry started from virtually nowhere early in the decade and, by 1959, was producing more than $325 million worth of concentrates, most of it destined for export, and much of that earmarked for the production of nuclear weapons. Uranium enjoyed a guaranteed, government-backed market; the United States and Britain had contracted to buy as much as Canada could produce. It seemed impossible to lose.

Uranium City

Uranium City's first permanent buildings were the claim recorder's office and the government liquor store, but nearly everything else was portable. With no paving or plumbing, drinking water was hauled from the lake and sold for a dollar a barrel. Permanent buildings were hauled in too – the movie theatre, hospital, police station and jail were dragged across the frozen lake from the nearby ghost town of Goadsville.

The new town had a respectable section with prefab bungalows and the Anglican and Catholic churches at the top of a hill, but the more flavourful quarter was in the other section, where hundreds of people lived year-round in tents and perished intermittently when their camp stoves overheated. There were streets with names like Fission Avenue and Nuclear Avenue; plenty of cars, some of them flown in aboard DC6s; and about fifteen miles of unpaved road. The movies at the Uranium Theatre changed every second night, the beer parlour in the Uranium City Hotel was seldom empty and, on winter evenings, when the taxis waiting outside kept their motors running, the clouds of frozen exhaust almost enveloped the building.

Bartlett's Cafe had the city's only jukebox, and its records (including "Long Tall Sally" by Elvis Presley) were changed once a year. You could buy almost anything at McIver's General Store: the ceiling was hung with chemical toilets, rubber boots and dogsled harnesses; the bacon was sold in slabs stacked near the stove; and the beans were dished out from huge bins near the counter.

There were dances in the basement of the Catholic church, softball games in the summer among teams from the mines and, in winter, high-school dances that were enlivened by students who dumped the coke out of their bottles and filled them with straight rye. "Most of the time we'd dance to records," recalls a graduate of Uranium City High School, "but sometimes we'd have a band consisting of banjo and piano. The dances took place in a cleared-out classroom, and most of the kids who came were very tough. Black leather jackets and mukluks were standard for the boys, and polkas and square dances were the favourites. The kids ran the school, so there was necking and God knows what else in the classrooms, and of course there was plenty of drinking."

$1,200 a month

It was the same story in Elliot Lake, Ontario, centre of an even bigger uranium strike in 1954. At the boom's peak, there were eleven mines in the Elliot Lake-Blind River area, including Consolidated Denison, the world's largest, whose reserves were twice as large as all the American producers put together. By 1956, Elliot Lake had built hundreds of modern suburban-style bungalows, but the approaches to the town were lined with tents, trailers and shacks, the Toronto-Dominion bank operated out of a converted house, the dentist and hairdresser were housed in trailers,

Alfred Valdmanis

Joey Smallwood's financial wizard, Latvian economist Alfred Valdmanis, was hired to remake the island of Newfoundland from a fishing post into an industrial power. He gave building contracts to firms crazy or courageous enough to invest in Newfoundland and, for three years, he was the second most powerful man in the province. In 1954, he was convicted of extorting $470,000 and given four years at hard labour.

One Damn Thing After Another

$26,000 Reward

EDWIN ALONZO BOYD, Alias Chas. B. HUNTER; alias Charles HUNTER; alias Jack THOMPSON; alias John HAWKINS, Age 37. 5'7⅜". Slim build. Black hair (grey). Blue eyes. Fresh comp.

WILLIAM RUSSELL JACKSON, alias A. GIBSON, Age 25. 5'7½". Medium build. Dk. br. hair. Blue eyes. Medium comp. "Eleanor" Tatooed right forearm.

LEONARD JACKSON, alias Robert KENT, Age 29, 5'9½". Medium build. Dk. br. Hair. Brown eyes. Dark Comp. Left foot artificial (limps).

VALENT LESSO alias Steve SUCHAN; alias Victor J. LENNOFF, Age 24. 5'10". Medium build. Brown hair. Brown eyes. Medium comp. Face pimply and pock-marked.

September 7, 1952: *Charged with armed robbery and murder, the Boyd Gang escapes from Toronto's Don Jail.*

October 16, 1954: *Hurricane Hazel hits central Ontario, flooding homes, roads and crops. The damages for Canada's worst recorded hurricane total $100 million and 80 fatalities are recorded.*

May 5, 1950: *Flood waters of the Red River inundate 600 square miles around Winnipeg as 100,000 people are evacuated from their homes.*

June 17, 1958: *The Second Narrows Bridge across Vancouver's Burrard Inlet collapses. A mistake in arithmetic is blamed for 18 deaths and 20 injuries.*

October 23, 1958: *Explosions in the coal mines at Springhill, Nova Scotia, claim 74 lives. Two years previously, a similar explosion had claimed 39.*

August 15, 1953: *The Kingston Pen erupts as chanting inmates protesting a cancelled baseball game burn three buildings and cause $2 million damage.*

July 15, 1950: *The 20,000-ton liner* Franconia *runs aground off the Ile d' Orléans in the St. Lawrence River on its way from Quebec City to Liverpool.*

In February 1947, the first of 1,278 wells in Alberta's fabulous Leduc oil field "came in." The American capital that subsequently poured into Alberta oil and Labrador iron created most of the prosperity that Canadians came to take for granted in the next ten years.

and the high school consisted of three curtained-off rooms in the recreation hall. Mine-shaft drillers were earning as much as $1,200 a month, but it was dangerous work. In eleven months of 1956, twenty-six men were killed underground.

The road between Elliot Lake and Blind River was legendary. In the spring of 1957, the twenty-mile trip from the highway took about five hours, and some trucks were known to have taken as long as two days. "Every time it rained," a taxi driver reported, "you'd see 30 cars stuck in the mud."

"insulbrick and clapboard"

This hysteria had been almost continuous since 1947, when Imperial Oil's fabulous Leduc strike launched the Alberta oil and gas boom. Before Leduc, Red Water was a sleepy town northeast of Edmonton with three grain elevators, two garages, no drugstore, no bank, no indoor plumbing, no street lights and a population of 160. By 1950 the population had jumped to 3,500 – most of them housed in shacks and trailers on the edge of town – and progress came in the form of a new hotel, four new stores, three lumberyards, two banks, two cinemas, a dance hall, a drugstore, a post office, nineteen street lights, daily milk delivery, a full time policeman and local branches of the Board of Trade and Youth for Christ.

Red Water was typical of the boom's impact on the West. In Fort St. John, British Columbia, centre of an oil and gas exploration spree in 1957, the population jumped from 2,300 to 4,000 in a single year. A visiting reporter named Pierre Berton described it as "a jungle of insulbrick and clapboard, no-vacancy signs and help-wanted placards, clustered trailers and broken plank sidewalks, half-erected buildings and crowded Chinese restaurants, all stuck together by a mucilage of gumbo and propelled by fierce optimism, hard drink and fast money." Like most of the instant

BOOM TOWNS

Although copper had been discovered in Flin Flon (above) as early as 1915, it was not until the booming fifties that the electrical industries created an insatiable demand for the ore. Meanwhile, tent cities (below) pushed further and further into the bleak bush of Labrador, sheltering the 10,000 men who mined Ungava's iron wealth for shipment to southern smelters.

communities that the oil boom created, Fort St. John was a town planner's nightmare, but nobody cared. "Maybe it is ugly," said Ma Murray, editor of the Alaska *Highway News,* "but by God, it's progressive ugliness."

Ma Murray

Editor and publisher of the weekly *Alaska Highway News,* Ma Murray delivered smiles and chuckles and hard-boiled opinion to many readers in British Columbia's north. Born in 1888, the scrappy and outspoken Margaret Teresa Lally Murray combined wisdom plus invective into a journalistic style that was at home in the fast-buck energy of the frontier.

"a twentieth-century New Town"

When the Aluminum Company of Canada, early in the decade, planned its townsite at Kitimat, 400 lonely miles up the coast from Vancouver, it was determined to avoid this chaotic form of development. The company's vast hydroelectric and aluminum smelter project was to cost $600 million, and would eventually support a city of 50,000 people. Alcan decided to do things right and spent nearly a quarter of a million dollars on advance planning of what *Architectural Forum* called "the first complete twentieth-century New Town in North America."

On paper it looked lovely. There was no main street, no downtown, no slums, and it was the planners' proud boast that, since the town's suburban streets had been so cunningly arranged, no Kitimat child would have to cross a street to get to school. Allowing for Kitimat's 87-inch annual rainfall, there were plenty of breezeways and covered terraces. Since the smelter's potlines would run twenty-four hours a day, the Alcan planners placed the master bedrooms in all the houses away from childrens' play areas, so that shift workers could get some sleep in the daytime. Place names were controlled by the planners too, so that one neighbourhood had all its streets named after birds – including Gander Crescent, Gannet Crescent, Partridge Street and Petrel Street. Alcan also hired a company recreation director.

The vision, in other words, was of a tidy suburban community that would materialize overnight in the middle of the wilderness. Much to their credit, however, the town's residents persisted in behaving like people. Some liked the place; others loathed it. "Some people," observed Mayor Wilbur Hallman, "think we ought to have slums for those who want them." There were innumerable soccer teams, a twenty-member symphony orchestra, art clubs, handicraft circles, service clubs and a literary society. But they could not fully disguise the fact that it rained nearly all the time, the cost of living was high, there was a desperate shortage of unattached women and, apart from working, there was really very little to do. It is not surprising that by 1957 a Vancouver hotelier had seen fit to establish, in a town of fourteen thousand people, the nation's largest beer parlour.

from boom to bust

But booms invariably lead to busts, and the galloping prosperity that characterized such towns as Kitimat, Elliot Lake and Uranium City was marred by the fickleness of world markets and the gnawing suspicion that foreign contracts for uranium would not be renewed. Some saw it coming. "We have temporary bunkhouses, temporary churches, temporary stores, temporary girlfriends. Everything is temporary except the mines, and some say they're temporary too," mused an engineer in Elliot Lake in the mid-fifties.

They were, in a way. One black day in 1959 the United States decided to stop stockpiling uranium. Then came the corollary of the boom – the instant bust that threatened the uranium towns with extinction.

By 1959, most Canadians realized that the prosperity that had given the decade so much of its flavour had some serious limitations. For one thing, booms tend sooner or later to become busts. For another, it became apparent that much of our prosperity had been achieved at the expense of our economic independence.

DOMINION DAY ISSUE
The Mounties—FIRST OF FIVE PARTS
Ottawa—A PORTFOLIO OF RARE PHOTOGRAPHS
MACLEAN'S
JULY 1 1954 CANADA'S NATIONAL MAGAZINE 15 CENTS

Rex Woods lampoons Canada's perennial flag controversy on the Dominion Day issue, 1954.

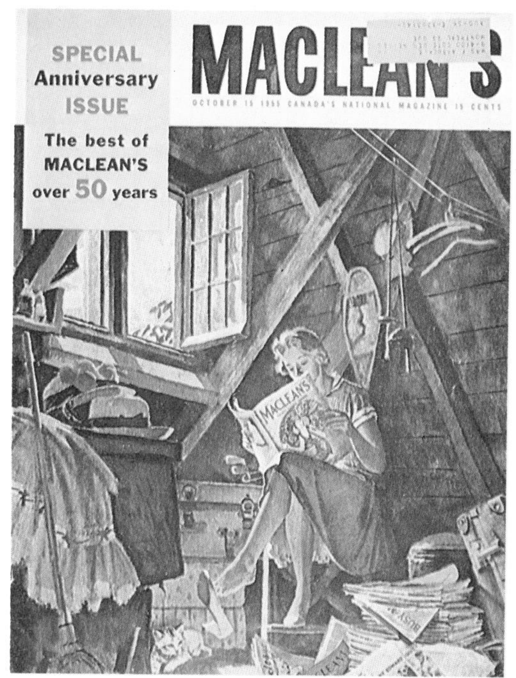

Artist Franklin Arbuckle's daughter peruses back issues on the 50th anniversary cover.

How *Maclean's* Saw the Fifties

With its roster of award-winning journalists and artists, *Maclean's* was both a mirror to the past and a guide to the future. Throughout the fifties, the magazine covered everything from the underworld in Montreal to the revolutionary new birth control pill and an eye-witness report from war-torn southern Korea. Staff members unearthed a priceless collection of negatives by William Notman, and the "Flashback" explored curiosities from our past.

GOING STEADY
Is it ruining our teen-agers?
Toronto the Gay: fine food, a night-life boom
CLYDE GILMOUR PICKS THE BEST MOVIES OF 1958
MACLEAN'S
JANUARY 3 1959 CANADA'S NATIONAL MAGAZINE 15 CENTS

All eyes are glued to "Hockey Night in Canada" this Saturday night in a Quebec fishing hut.

Workers on Ed McNally's DEW-line trace an unidentified foreign craft on Christmas Eve.

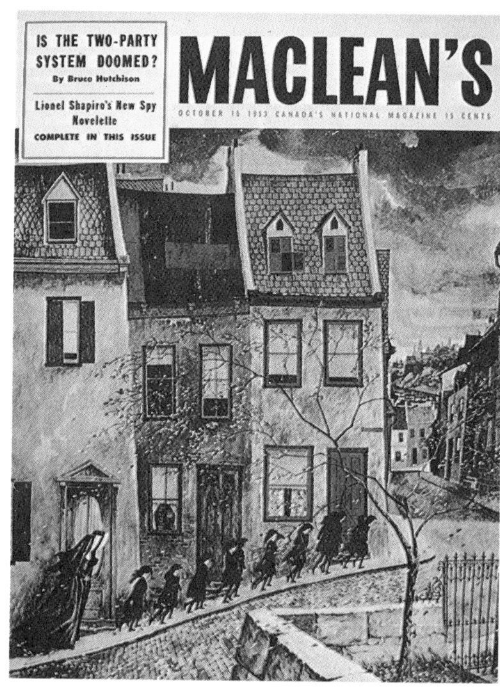

The sisters escort Quebec schoolchildren along the windy streets to morning mass.

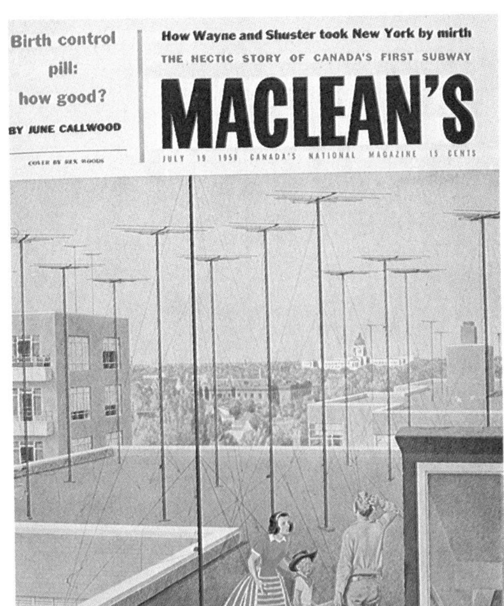

A forest of TV antennas bears witness to the nation's passionate love affair with the tube.

A crestfallen junior leaguer is handed a two-minute penalty for some fancy high sticking.

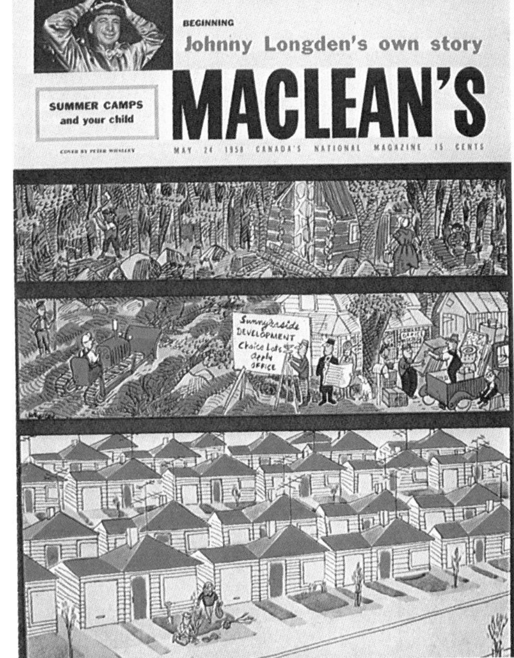

The wry wit of Peter Whalley telescopes one hundred years of progress in Canadian housing.

William Winter's Toronto Stock Exchange by day and night – the two sides of the coin.

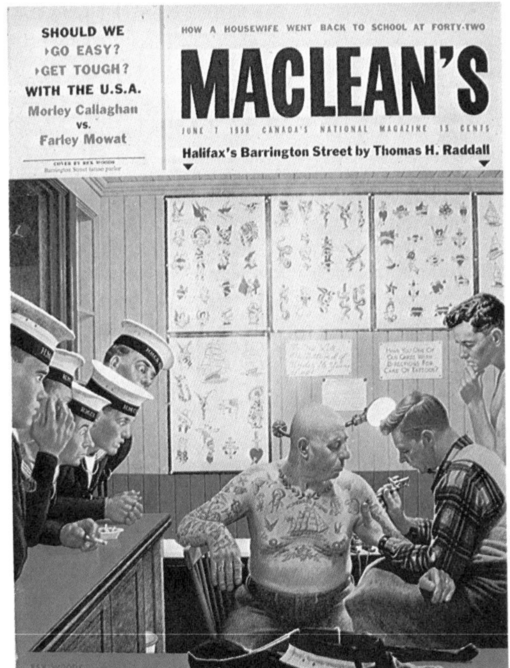

Sailors from all over the world still flock to this Barrington St. parlour in Halifax.

Ed McNally's "reflection" in 1958 represents an innovation in the decade's commercial art.

Maple leaves rain on Oscar Cahen's three jolly hunters returning with their weekend spoils.

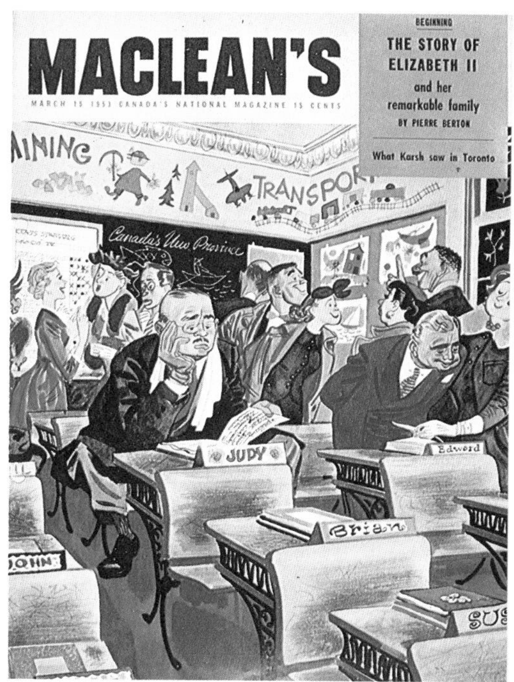

Parents' Night in a crowded classroom of the baby boom draws the eager and the perplexed.

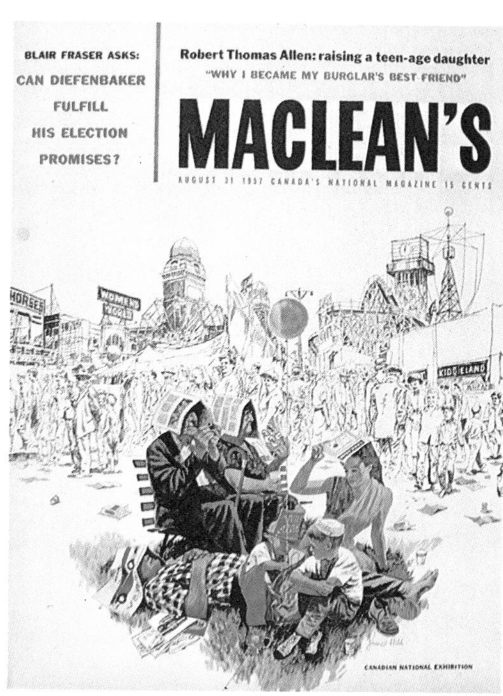

James Hill shows three generations after a trek through the raucous midway at the CNE.

Even John Little caught Grey Cup fever as the Eskimos and Alouettes fight to the finish.

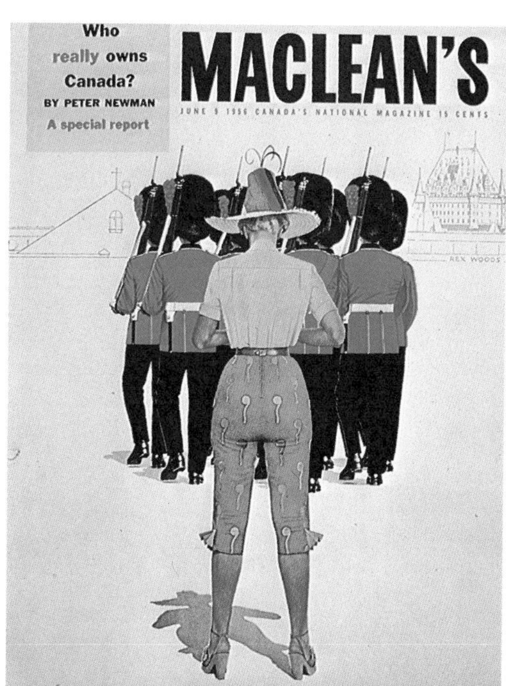

Toreador pants and dress uniforms vie in Rex Woods' unique perspective on Parliament Hill.

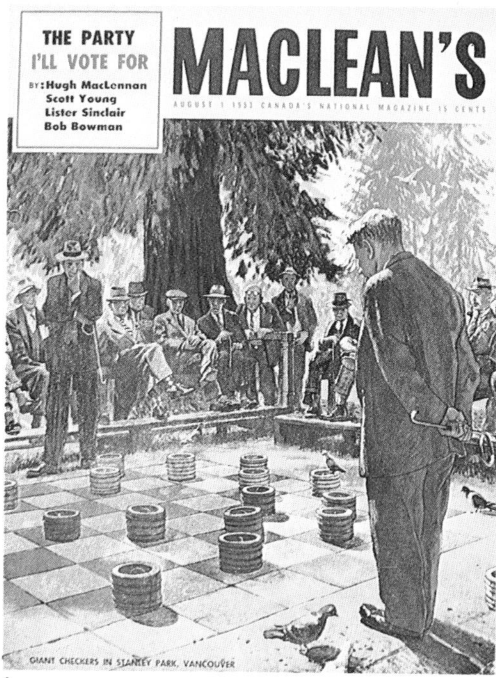

An old man quietly plots his next move in a game of checkers in Vancouver's Stanley Park.

An open hand and a smart blue uniform. This RCAF recruiting poster had an attractive pitch for the hundreds who signed up in the fifties.

CHAPTER SEVEN

How We Met the Red Menace

. . . empty pews and empty churches mark an easy prey to a fanatic, soulless communism.

Advertisement of Canadair Limited, 1955

There was something about him that could only have been Canadian: scholarly and gracious, but without an Oxbridge accent; familiar with the uses of power, yet distinctly un-American at a time when the Americans seemed to have inherited the earth; deeply religious, but in a personal, internal way. His name was Herbert Norman and he was a Canadian diplomat, one of the most brilliant and accomplished men in an External Affairs Department that was becoming recognized as perhaps the ablest diplomatic service in the world.

Now, early on the morning of April 4, 1957, he was standing on the roof of an apartment house, pacing nervously back and forth and looking out across the hot Egyptian cityscape to the sky beyond. He then sat down on the parapet and put his head in his hands. By this time people in the street had begun to notice the strange behaviour of the man on the roof. A crowd gathered. Norman got up, took off his jacket, carefully folded it – he'd always been scrupulously neat – and laid it on the parapet. It was only when he took off his watch and glasses and laid them beside his jacket that a woman below screamed: "He's going to jump!" He fell feet first and died instantly when he hit the ground.

Norman had been the victim of anti-Communist attacks since 1951, when a witness before the United States Senate Subcommittee on Internal Security had accused him of pro-Communist sympathies. The charges persisted throughout the 1950s in speeches, newspaper articles, pamphlets and in testimony before the proliferating organizations, both public and private, that were capitalizing on the political psychosis that came to be known as McCarthyism. Though the attacks were standard smears, baseless and vaguely worded, they tortured Norman. One of the world's leading authorities on Japanese history, he was a man of almost Oriental sensitivity. When the attacks began, he offered to resign, but External Affairs Minister Lester Pearson affirmed his confidence in the diplomat. When the smears persisted, Norman told his wife: "Why must I go through that again? I've become an embarrassment to my government."

Norman was the most conspicuous Canadian victim of the anti-Communist hysteria that was characteristic of the period. But his death and his life constituted an encouraging commentary on the different political climates that prevailed on either side of the forty-eighth parallel. Norman was a man of moderation and sensibility, an exemplar of what we were coming to regard as the pre-eminent Canadian virtues. And though he was a victim of McCarthyism, as surely as if his persecutors had

Canada's RCAF tailor-made a training programme for women in the decade.

Herbert Norman

On April 4, 1957, haunted by charges that he was a Communist sympathizer, Canadian diplomat Herbert Norman fell to his death from the roof of a Cairo hotel. Born and raised in Japan, the son of missionary parents, Norman had distinguished himself as a brilliant scholar. His reputation as an acute interpreter of international affairs gained him access to world leaders of every colour and persuasion. Yet his death remains shrouded in mystery. Did Norman take his own life or was he pushed? We may never know.

physically pushed him off that Cairo rooftop, he was one of Canada's very few such victims. While most of the United States worked itself into a dither over threats of Soviet expansion and internal subversion, Canadians remained relatively immune to hysteria.

During the decade, the United States produced Senator Joe McCarthy who terrorized the whole country with his charges of Communist interests, a columnist named Westbrook Pegler who advocated the death penalty for membership in the Communist Party, an American Legion faction that suspected the Girl Scouts of Communist infiltration, and a member of the Indiana Textbook Commission named Mrs. Thomas J. Hoyt who demanded in 1953 that *Robin Hood* be removed from the schools because the story "promotes Communist doctrine."

the "cold war"

In this same period, although Canada had its share of anti-Communist zealots, they never became a factor in the political process. Instead, we tended to treat Soviet imperialism for what it was: abroad, a genuine threat to world peace; at home, a problem that called for watchfulness, but not hysteria.

Prime Minister Louis St. Laurent set the tone in his New Year's Day message in 1950. The year before, he had described the world situation as "very grave," and had spoken of war as "possible, though not inevitable." During 1949, he now said, new reasons for uneasiness had appeared. He called the Communist takeover in China "the greatest victory for totalitarianism and defeat for democracy since the Russian Revolution." His tone was solemn, and it seemed appropriate.

Canadians, who had so recently finished with one war, had become accustomed to living in the grim expectation of another. A 1951 Gallup poll indicated that, although only 45 per cent of the population had heard of the term "cold war," 36 per cent believed that an enemy attack on Canada was imminent. In some parts of the country, the proportion of frightened citizens ran as high as 50 per cent. In the summer of 1950, when smoke from Alberta forest fires drifted eastward, police switchboards received hundreds of calls from people asking if The Bomb had fallen. In 1951, when a synthetic rubber plant in Sarnia exploded in the middle of the night, thousands of panicky residents, most of them still in pyjamas, rushed out into the streets, certain that war had finally come.

Russia's acquisition of the atomic bomb in 1949, together with the revelations of the Gouzenko spy trials, had already prepared most Canadians for the worst. When, on June 25, 1950, Communist troops swarmed across the thirty-eighth parallel into South Korea, it could have been the signal for cross-country panic and hysteria. It could have been except for the fact that Canadians, at least in crises where Britain was not involved, were remarkably susceptible to counsels of moderation. Indeed, Ottawa's response bordered on the phlegmatic.

Korea

When UN Secretary General Trygve Lie issued his July 14 appeal for ground forces to curb North Korean aggression, St. Laurent was off fishing. Five days later the cabinet considered the request and decided to contribute transport planes and three destroyers, but no troops. The following month the government reversed itself: troops would be recruited for Korean service after all. By the end of August, eight thousand had volunteered. Comparatively, Canada ranked third among the members of the United Nations in her aid to South Korea.

The following November the first advance

Canada's Forgotten War

Over twenty-two thousand Canadians fought in Korea for three years and helped keep the uneasy peace for an additional two. Yet Korea created hardly a ripple in public opinion and remains a forgotten war.

Covering Korea for Maclean's, *Pierre Berton snapped this picture of two Canadian privates.*

Armed, gas-masked, Canadian guards supervise POWs on "honey-bucket" detail at Compound 66.

The 2nd Battalion of the Queen's Own Rifles rest after a battalion attack at Nightmare Range in 1954, during a shaky Korean truce.

party of Canadians reached Pusan to make housekeeping arrangements for the brigade that would follow. The Princess Pats were fighting in the front line by February of 1952, but the remaining two battalions did not leave their training base at Fort Lewis, Washington, until the following April.

Despite a tardy arrival, the Canadians fought some of the fiercest skirmishes of the three-year war. Nearly 25,000 of them saw service before the 1953 truce, and they formed part of a Commonwealth Division that was heavily exposed to the nastiness of an Asian land war.

Canadair was the leading producer of jet aircraft in Canada. This 1956 ad touts their F-86 Sabre Jet. The RCAF equipped an entire air division with F-86s as part of its contribution to the "Wings of Nato."

hair-raising heroism

Although there were no great battles for the Canadians in Korea, and no victories that captured public imagination at home, there were individual acts of hair-raising heroism. When groundfire wounded the pilot of an American reconnaissance plane north of Seoul, the Canadian observer who was aboard for training, Captain Joseph Tremblay, somehow managed to steer the plane back to Seoul for a crash landing, then dragged the wounded pilot from the flaming wreckage. Another army man, Corporal Kenneth McOrmond, was hit by Chinese mortar fragments and left for dead by withdrawing troops of the 25th Infantry Brigade. When advancing Chinese soldiers found him during the night, McOrmond was fully conscious, but played dead. The troops rifled his pockets for souvenirs, then plunged a bayonet into his ribs, clubbed him with a rifle butt and fired at him with a machine-pistol. The bayonet and bullets both penetrated McOrmond's heavy parka, but just missed his body. At dawn, he crawled back to the Canadian line, to an incredulous welcome from his company.

On the home front, although some Canadians tried to remember that the fighting was going on and although the IODE sent gifts and food parcels, most ignored the war. When the Vancouver *Sun* tested reader interest by running the same Korean dispatch on the front page three days in a row, nobody noticed. About the only people who seemed alarmed by the war, in fact, were French Canadians, who feared a new threat of conscription. *Montreal-Matin,* a pro-Duplessis organ, asked: "Why cover with the name of a crusade the reflex action of the Anglo-Saxon world when its material interests are threatened?" *Le Devoir* was more succinct: "What are we doing in all this?"

Some Canadians, however, were less apathetic about fighting Communism at home. Rhys Sale, president of the Ford Motor Company's Canadian subsidiary, publicly urged in 1951 that the Communist Party of Canada again be outlawed. "There are some 30,000 Communists in Canada," he told the Toronto Canadian Club. "What a fine Trojan horse if we come to a showdown with the Joe Stalin mob!" Sale's speech drew many congratulatory letters and widespread editorial applause. But it won no compliance from the St. Laurent government, whose anti-Communist measures throughout the 1950s were appropriately watchful.

"disaffection of disloyalty"

In 1951, the Citizenship Act was amended to permit revocation of the citizenship of naturalized Canadians who had been convicted of offences involving "disaffection or disloyalty" to the Crown. The amendment was clearly aimed at Fred Rose, a naturalized Canadian and former Member of Parliament who had been convicted as a Soviet spy in 1946. The St. Laurent government also ordered security checks for all seamen serving on Canadian ships in the Great Lakes. After Mrs. Nora Rodd, a Windsor lawyer's wife, visited Moscow and Korea on a junket sponsored by the Canadian Congress of Women and began denouncing UN "atrocities" over Moscow Radio, the government broadened the definition of treason in the Criminal Code to include "assisting, while in or out of Canada, any enemy at war with Canada . . . whether or not a state of war exists."

"the Diefenbunker"

While Mrs. Rodd and other Soviet apologists never suffered from overt government interference, this didn't mean they were popular. When Dr. James Endicott, a former United Church missionary in China, returned home with the charges that UN forces were using germ warfare in Korea, he was booed at public meetings, denounced in scores of newspaper editorials and given a none-too-subtle warning by Justice Minister Stuart Garson. "The activities of such men," the minister assured Parliament, "are kept under constant surveillance." In 1953, when the so-called "Red Dean" of Canterbury, Dr. Hewlett Johnston, attempted to instruct students at the University of Western Ontario in the virtues of Stalinism, they pelted the seventy-nine-year-old man with fruit, threw stink-bombs, rang cowbells and eventually drove him from the hall.

In the early fifties, when the threat of instant extermination seemed very real, such reactions did not seem excessive. Just how real the threat appeared can be seen from the official attention that was paid to civil defence. The theory, which has never been repudiated by defence officials but which is scarcely mentioned any more, was that an urban population, if adequately prepared, can survive a nuclear attack. To this end, the government in 1950 undertook to co-ordinate national civil defence planning, and to assist provinces and municipalities in setting up their own CD programmes.

One element of the CD programme was evacua-

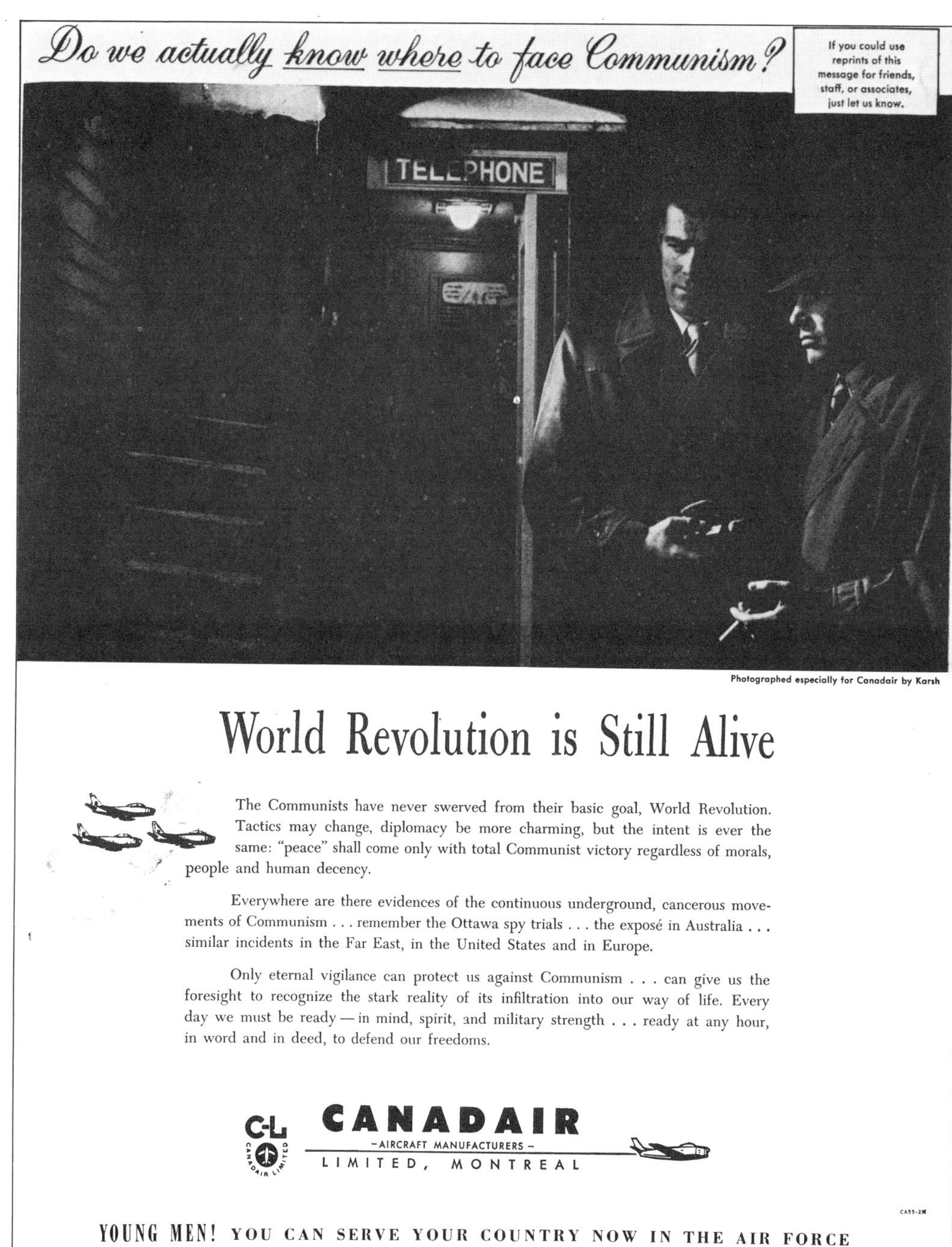

The "Cold War" occasionally generated considerable heat, as in this 1955 ad. Rumours of subversion and the reality of the Gouzenko case put any alien in a raincoat under suspicion.

The sleek Avro Arrow on the tarmac before the government decided to scrap the project and, with it, thirteen thousand jobs.

tion. At the behest of the local CD director, one physician in New Westminster, British Columbia, carried a crate of canned goods around in the trunk of his Oldsmobile for years, ready to race for the hinterland as soon as the order was given. It was never explained how he would get across the Pattulo Bridge if the bomb had blown it up. Ottawa's CD headquarters took the view that the island of Montreal could be evacuated in two hours, an estimate that most rush-hour motorists found optimistic in the extreme.

Another feature of the CD plan was the fall-out shelter. No one knows how many actually were built during the 1950s. By the end of the decade, only forty-one building permits for shelters had been granted, but estimates of how many were built without authorization ranged as high as three thousand. The best-known was the pink-walled retreat that John Diefenbaker built in 1959 just outside Ottawa; joyously, the press nicknamed it "The Diefenbunker." A Toronto *Star* reporter built a home-made shelter in a dream home in Etobicoke. The Toronto *Telegram,* as its CD contribution, had a reporter and his wife hole themselves up in a basement shelter for 168 hours. Two promoters from Vancouver toured the country publicizing a length of concrete drainpipe that they had converted into an all-purpose family fall-out shelter. It was equipped with oxygen tanks and encased in a perforated steel shield, housed four people comfortably and sold for $750.

Shelters were essentially a fad, and most Canadians regarded them as a huge joke. But they did underscore the sobering fact that Canada, shortly after the Korean balloon went up, was getting off to a fast start in the international arms race. In February 1951, Defence Minister Brooke Claxton announced that the government would spend $5 billion over the next three years on a military build-up unprecedented in peacetime.

The secrecy with which that money was spent was also unprecedented. In 1952, the Parliamentary Committee on Defence Expenditures was asked to approve an item worth $670 million. The information the committee was given was brief enough to quote in full: "Supplier, various; description, aircraft; date of order, various; number of units, classified." No questions were permitted.

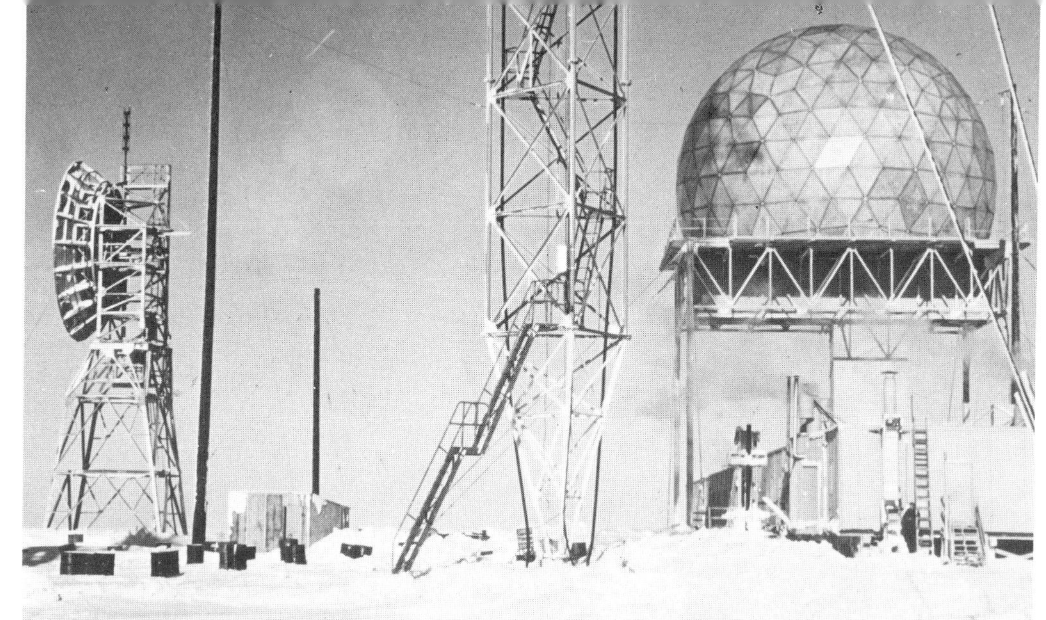

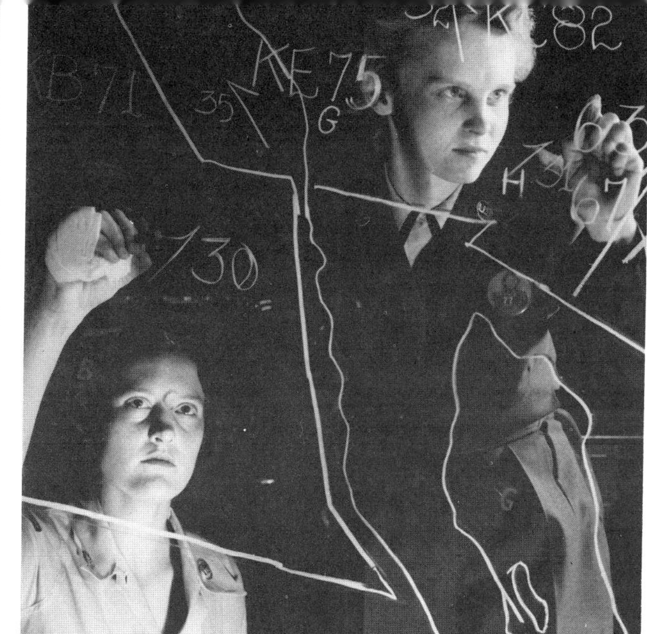

Disc-shaped radar (left) in Canada's north transmitted DEW-line sightings to NORAD headquarters in Colorado (right).

In this climate, it is hardly surprising that the armed services made some beguilingly silly purchases. The army spent $88,000 on 29,630 aluminum teapots, before somebody realized that most messes dispensed their tea from cafeteria-style urns. The navy ordered enough hatbands to last twenty-seven years, and then, no doubt detecting a further increase in cold war tension, ordered another 870,000, for a total cost to the taxpayer of $667,000.

Probably the least felicitous act of procurement, however, was the decision to build the Avro Arrow, a supersonic jet fighter that cost at least $400 million to develop. It was one of the fastest, most sophisticated manned aircraft ever built, but the prototype never went into production. The Diefenbaker government cancelled the order in 1958 because there were not enough orders to cover the costs. Its replacement, for the task of repelling Soviet nuclear bombers, was the American-developed Bomarc missile. It was the Diefenbaker government's unwillingness to accept the nuclear warheads for this weapon that eventually led to Diefenbaker's downfall.

By mid-decade, Canadian defence commitments extended halfway across the world and were swallowing an awesome proportion of the taxpayer's dollar – 40 per cent of the federal budget in 1955 and 1956. The Royal Canadian Air Force, as its NATO commitment in Europe, had twelve squadrons based in France and Belgium. Canadian army forces had been part of a NATO contingent stationed in Germany since the early 1950s, and we shared responsibility, and part of the cost, with the United States for North American air defence.

Probably the most controversial aspect of this commitment was our participation in the DEW (Distant Early Warning) Line, a three-tiered radar detection system strung across the far north that was designed to give advance warning of a Soviet attack. Canada's contribution was $320 million, but this was only part of the cost. We also effectively ceded to the United States sovereignty over large tracts of Canadian territory. Nominally, the DEW-line installations stood on Canadian soil, or to be precise, on Canadian muskeg, but access was quite properly restricted and responsibility for enforcing these restrictions rested with American

"The longest legs on TV," Sandra O'Neill was the star attraction for these two Canadian sergeants when the CBC *Concert Party troupe pulled into their lonely outpost on the Sinai.*

authorities. On the first press tour of the new system in 1956, Canadian reporters first had to fly to New York, then agree to have their copy censored by American authorities, then pass American security tests and accept American travel authorization—to visit their own country!

It is possible, just as the strategists tell us, that all these staggeringly expensive measures during the 1950s saved North America from a Soviet nuclear attack. But it is also tempting to assess exactly what we lost by spending billions of dollars to ward off an attack that never came.

the DEW-line

Thousands of men lived like sub-arctic moles to build the DEW-line installations, and invariably returned south with several thousand dollars in the bank. The decision to develop the Avro Arrow created a major-league aeronautics industry in Canada; and with the decision to scrap the project, several thousand jobs evaporated. The American decision to participate in the construction of the St. Lawrence Seaway was at least partly dictated by defence considerations. When the Pentagon switched from manned bombers to missiles, it reduced the demand for aluminum and delayed the planned expansion of the Kitimat smelter project. By the end of the decade, the significance of developments such as these had become uncomfortably clear.

In our haste to arm ourselves against the red menace and in our businesslike desire to sell the Americans raw materials for the same purpose, we managed to place our economy, our well-being, and much of our national livelihood in a state of inglorious dependence on the whims of American military strategy. If this was really the price of avoiding nuclear incineration in the 1950s, it was a good bargain. But if the threat was exaggerated, it was a very bad bargain indeed.

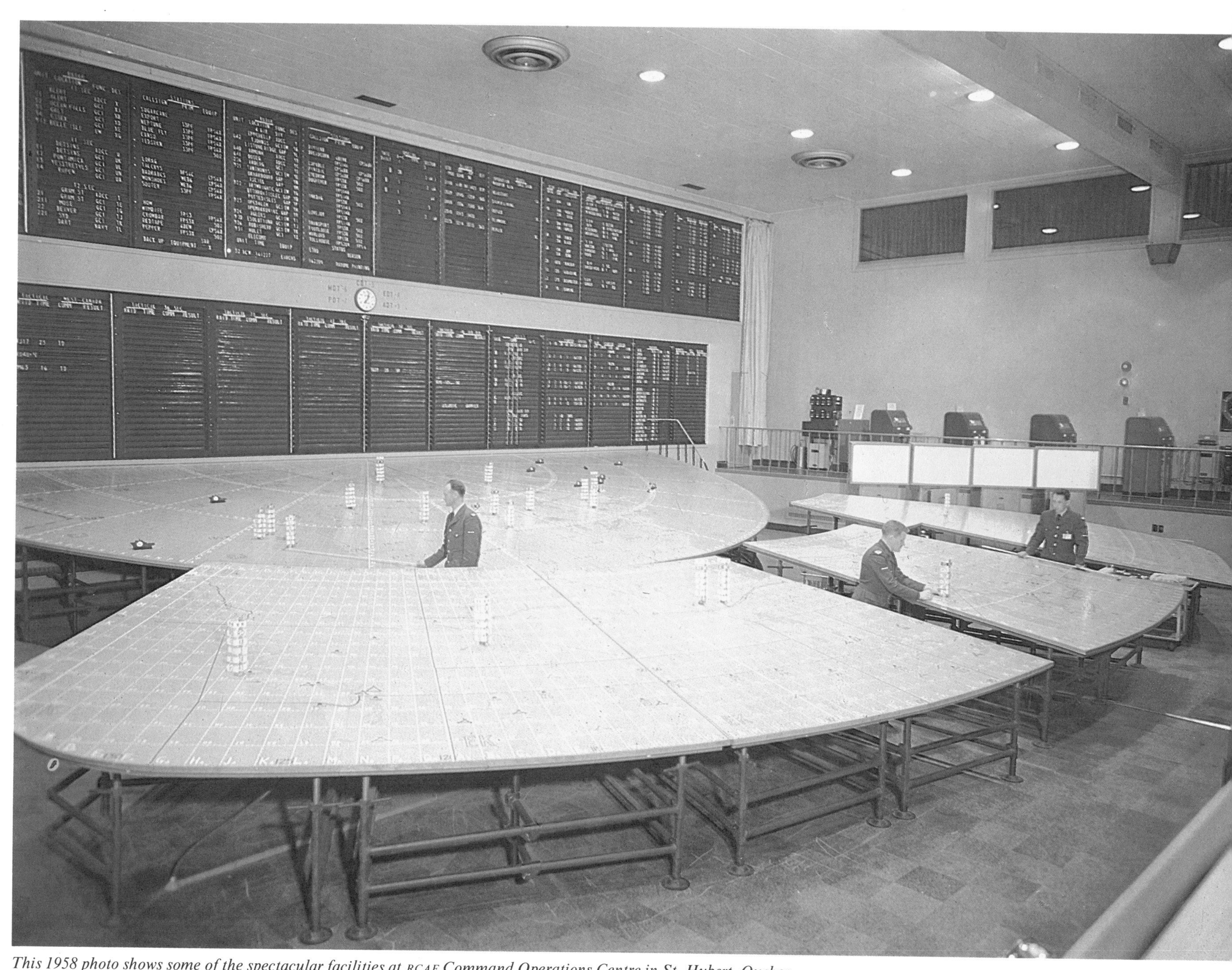

This 1958 photo shows some of the spectacular facilities at RCAF *Command Operations Centre in St. Hubert, Quebec. The* COC *controlled all interceptor aircraft and DEW-line information was constantly received and updated by teletype.*

Those Fabulous Flying Frenchmen

For five years in a row, from 1956 to 1960, jubilant Montreal Canadiens sipped champagne from the Stanley Cup. The Habs were established in 1909, eight years before the National Hockey League itself. Under the care of men like Frank Selke and Toe Blake, the Habs have known greater moments of triumph than any other team. In the fifties, the Canadiens and the Stanley Cup seemed inseparable and every youngster wanted a complete set of Canadiens bubble gum cards.

Emile Bouchard, defense.

Doug Harvey, defense.

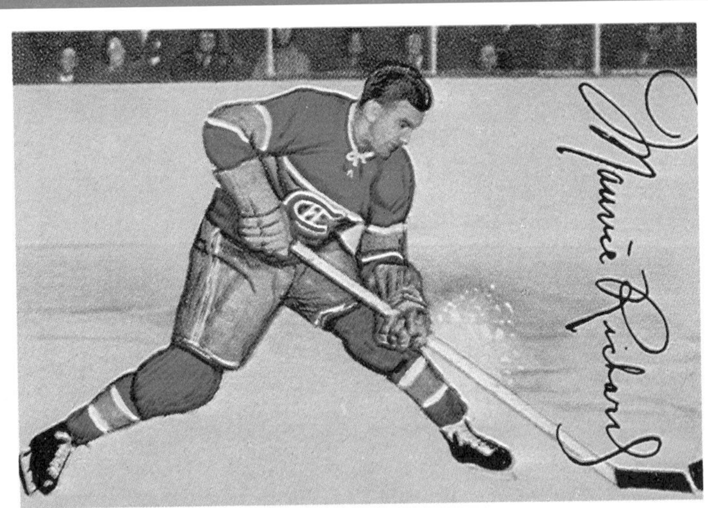

Maurice "The Rocket" Richard, r. wing and team captain.

Bernie Geoffrion, r. wing.

Jean Beliveau, centre.

Marshall, r. wing; Henri Richard, centre; Moore, l. wing.

Floyd Curry, forward.

Dollard St. Laurent, defense.

Provost, r. wing; Goyette, centre; Pronovost, l. wing.

Elmer Lach, centre.

Bert Olmstead, l. wing.

CHAPTER EIGHT

The Private Kingdom of Quebec

I have no family. My only responsibility is the welfare of Quebec. I belong to the province.

Maurice Duplessis, Premier of Quebec

For nearly a week he lay dying, shielded from the world by protective layers of cabinet ministers, executive assistants, public relations men, worried doctors and company cops. He lay in a white iron bed, in a hospital owned by the company that owned the town that sat in the middle of a vast and lonely wilderness of gaunt trees and slate-grey skies, a wilderness where the earth was almost red because there was so much iron in it. Wily old Maurice Le Noblet Duplessis, who had ruled Quebec for nearly two decades, had come to see Schefferville – a town that only a few years earlier he had helped to create. And now the man of iron was dying in the town that iron built.

He died almost secretly, like an ancient king trying to shield his subjects from the awesome fact of his mortality. Two days after the local parish priest had administered the rites of extreme unction, a government spokesman in Quebec City would confirm only that the premier had suffered "a serious indisposition." In the early hours of the morning of September 7, 1959, he died. For the three days it took to bury him, his remains were the object of a flood of public grief. The people of Quebec, tens of thousands of them, wept as they shuffled past his bronze coffin and crossed themselves as the cortège wound through the autumn streets. They loved this old man, loved him in a way that Duplessis himself had never loved anyone. And when the people of Quebec wept at his passing, they were weeping for a part of themselves.

Maurice Duplessis *was* Quebec in the 1950s, in the same way that Charles de Gaulle would be France a decade later. He was premier from 1936 to 1939, and again from 1944 until his death. During that period, he presided over a province and a people whose most basic political aim was *survivance:* the preservation of the French fact in an alien, Anglo-Saxon continent.

Quite obviously he succeeded – but at a price. Shut inside a defensive shell, French Canada remained a closed and repressive society, and the man who ruled it was able to assume arbitrary powers that few politicians in North America have possessed in this century.

When a pulp company displeased him, he passed a law, in flagrant violation of several hundred years of legal precedent, that retroactively doubled its taxes. When he decided that Quebec was imperilled by Communism, he invoked the infamous Padlock Law, which allowed the police to bar from occupancy any premises used for the

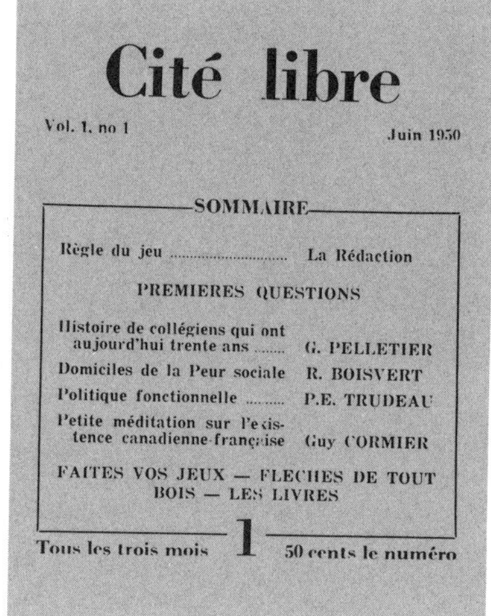

Cité libre

Vol. 1, no 1 — Juin 1950

SOMMAIRE

Règle du jeu .... La Rédaction

PREMIERES QUESTIONS

Histoire de collégiens qui ont aujourd'hui trente ans .... G. PELLETIER

Domiciles de la Peur sociale — R. BOISVERT

Politique fonctionnelle .... P.E. TRUDEAU

Petite méditation sur l'existence canadienne-française — Guy CORMIER

FAITES VOS JEUX — FLECHES DE TOUT BOIS — LES LIVRES

Tous les trois mois — 1 — 50 cents le numéro

In 1950, nine years before the death of Le Chef, *Quebec reform liberals united under the banner of* Cité Libre, *with notables Gérard Pelletier and Pierre Trudeau in the editorial ranks.*

Opposite page: *The hundred-car funeral procession of Maurice Duplessis wound its way through crowded streets from the Quebec City cathedral to his birth and burial place in busy Trois Rivières.*

purposes of spreading Communist propaganda. When he was criticized by a professor at some university, he would use his fiscal powers to try to get him fired. He ensured the subservience of most of the province's newspapers by forcing pulp and paper companies to sell their newsprint in Quebec at cut-rate prices.

In Catholic Quebec, there were few objections to his harassment of the Jehovah's Witnesses sect. Between 1946 and 1953, the Duplessis government launched more than sixteen hundred prosecutions against Witnesses, on charges that ranged from sedition to handing out pamphlets without a permit. Hundreds were arrested, jailed or roughed up, and dozens of Kingdom Halls were damaged by righteous Quebeckers, with a minimum of police interference and with Duplessis' tacit approval. He called the campaign against the sect "a war without mercy."

Paul-Emile Cardinal Léger

His Eminence Paul-Emile Cardinal Léger was one of the few Canadians ever to be elected to the College of Cardinals in Rome. He was born in St. Anicet, Quebec, in 1904, a son of the village merchant, and entered the priesthood in 1929. His rise in the church ranks was meteoric and he was consecrated Archbishop of Montreal in 1950, thereby becoming the spiritual leader of the second largest Catholic diocese in the world. In 1967, one of the most powerful leaders in the Church, he resigned to work with African lepers.

bogeymen of Quebec

He even inspired a joke, popular around 1958, that neatly defined his regime. A Montrealer asks a visitor from Switzerland, "Why does your country have a minister of the navy, and no navy?"

"Why not?" the Swiss replies. "Quebec's got a justice minister, hasn't it?"

Nearly all of Duplessis' "wars" were directed against external threats – atheists, Communists, centralizers. He was able to fight these bogeymen only because of the structure of Quebec society at the time, a society which still viewed change of any kind as a threat to its existence.

In the villages, the curé's word was seldom disobeyed. In the northern Quebec village of Ste. Germaine, the local postmaster was in the habit of turning over Baptist tracts that turned up in the mails to the local priest, who burned them. When charged with mail-tampering, the priest was unrepentant, even though disavowed by Cardinal Léger. The church hierarchy still spoke with massive authority on public questions and seldom disagreed with the government. Education was still firmly under parochial control, and the *collèges classiques* and universities were still not producing the graduates required for an increasingly technological society.

Under the 2,515-article Quebec Civil Code, women were still regarded almost as chattels. Girls could marry at twelve, boys at fourteen, although the same children were not allowed to see certain movies. A wife was not legally permitted to sell property, undergo surgery, sign contracts or launch lawsuits without her husband's permission.

protection of public morals

Families were still large and close-knit. Public dancing was forbidden in Trois Rivières as late as 1952. The 378-page manual prepared by the Roman Catholic Church as a textbook for prospective married couples counselled Quebec's future brides: "Girls should not wear high-heeled shoes. They are the cause of painful menstruation and many miscarriages." The manual added that "Much of the persistent discord in certain homes can be traced to the use of twin beds."

Church and state conspired to protect public morals. Archbishop (and later Cardinal) Léger in 1951 forbade all games of chance in his diocese, including bingo. Duplessis himself complained about films shown on television that were "repulsive to morals," and promised to censor them along with those shown in movie theatres. Among the films found to be repugnant was *Martin Luther;* it depicted the Pope in a bad light, the censor explained, and so would not be shown in theatres. "Whether or not the film is historically accurate is not the point," he added. No one was more vigilant than the Quebec authorities, sacred and secular, in policing racy books and magazines. In 1955, the town of Aylmer passed a law regulating "peace, order and good morals" that banned everything from swearing and fortune telling to roller skating on public streets.

Montreal provided a roaring contrast not only to the puritanism of rural Quebec, but to the rest of Canada. It was a wide-open city, one of the most sophisticated, most deliciously sinful in North America. Proper Anglo-Saxons thought of it as a capital of vice, but in a country with a deficiency of vices, Montreal was more of a national resource than a national disgrace. Prostitution, gambling and clip-joint night clubs constituted a major industry, and it was routine to deplore the municipal corruption that made this state of affairs possible.

Montreal was also the only place in Canada where it was possible to have fun in public after 10 P.M. Night clubs, the kind we now associate with 1930s Hollywood movies, were almost as common as the discotheques of a later era. At El Morocco, a club near the Montreal Forum which bore a close resemblance to its Manhattan namesake, patrons dressed in evening finery for a costly evening of dining, dancing, drinking and floor-show-watching. There was a society orchestra that played smooth music for golden couples who sipped champagne cocktails and made brittle conversation. The decor was pure Art Deco, and the atmosphere owed more to New York than it did to anything that came from Quebec.

berets and fishnet stockings

Other night spots had a more indigenous flavour. Near the Windsor Station there flourished a black neighbourhood, many of whose residents worked as redcaps for the CPR, and its jazz clubs were an important ingredient of the city's night life, just as Harlem's were in the New York of the 1920s and 1930s. At one such club, the Alberta

Parents of seventeen children (seven sets of twins and three loners), Rosa and Paul-Emile Tremblay of Alma, Quebec, had their hands full on this 1957 all-expense-paid trip to Niagara Falls. A monthly government cheque of $186 supplemented the family income of $63 per week.

While Torontonians travelled long distances seeking out the nightlife of Buffalo and New York, Quebeckers could enjoy hometown entertainment in scores of glittering nightclubs and after-hour spots. Jacques Normand and his troupe were favourites at St. Germain de Pres Club.

Lounge, a young black jazz pianist named Oscar Peterson displayed a genius that would later make his name as well known in Prague and Bangkok as it would be in Canada.

The legitimate clubs closed at 2 A.M., but that did not end the party. Downtown Montreal was studded with scores of "blind pigs," after-hours drinking spots where the carousing continued until early morning and the prostitutes, for the benefit of out-of-town conventioneers with fantasies, wore berets and fishnet stockings. Prostitution and blind pigs were, of course, illegal. They flourished, however, with the connivance of police and municipal authorities until 1954, when the reform administration of Jean Drapeau attempted to clean up the city and succeeded at least in making the vice industry slightly less conspicuous.

virtue rewarded and vice rebuked

Montreal's night life was essentially an alien phenomenon, however. Outside the big cities, Quebec's literature and popular culture still reflected the gloomy, Gothic character of Duplessis-land. In the small towns and villages of Quebec, melodramas that portrayed virtue rewarded and vice rebuked were unfailingly popular. One of the best-loved was called *La Petite Aurore,* which depicted the misfortunes of a ten-year-old girl who was cruelly mistreated by her stepmother. The play was based on an actual incident from the 1920s in which a young girl, Aurore Gagnon, died of maltreatment. It packed parish halls in rural Quebec until television killed it. Two filmed melodramas, *Couer de Maman* and *L'esprit du Mal,* were produced on a shoe-string budget in Montreal and grossed nearly $1 million on their first showings in rural Quebec. The real hero of both these dramas was the ordered family life of rural Quebec.

The literature of the period similarly reflected

the constricted quality of Quebec society, but in a less favourable light. The 1955 winner of Le Cercle du Livre de France award, for instance, was Jean Filiatrault's *Chaînes,* an oppressively gloomy collection of stories, one about two boys, the first emasculated by a possessive mother, the second brutalized by a domineering father. The first youth's mother goes mad and strangles her pet cat when the son leaves to get married. The father drives the second youth insane, and he kills his mother. Quebec novels, commented Le Cercle's chairman, "are obsessed with violence, tragedy and tormented introspection."

There were exceptions to this pattern. Gratien Gélinas became a Quebec folk hero with his portrayals of Fridolin, a waif-like, tramp-like, Chaplinesque character who, in an annual succession of popular stage revues, commented satirically and hilariously on Quebec life. French television flourished with a vigour and originality that was lacking in English-speaking Canada. The *chansonniers* became a force in Quebec popular music, in the same way folk singers such as Ian and Sylvia were becoming popular in English Canada.

by only two points

There was much pent-up feeling in Quebec, however, and occasionally it burst forth in frightening ways. In 1955, Montreal erupted when Clarence Campbell, president of the National Hockey League, benched Maurice "Rocket" Richard. Campbell's decision came at a crucial time; the Canadiens were leading the Detroit Red Wings by only two points at that stage of the season, and Richard was only two points ahead of his team-mate, Bernie "Boom Boom" Geoffrion, in the scoring race. (Geoffrion would surpass Richard during the suspension and beat him by one point.)

When Campbell gave Richard a season's sus-

VIVE RICHARD!

An egg-splattered Clarence Campbell (above) held onto his hat in the Montreal Forum minutes before the 1955 Richard Riot. Five years later, a more convivial Campbell congratulated Richard after the Canadians took the Stanley Cup for the fifth year in a row.

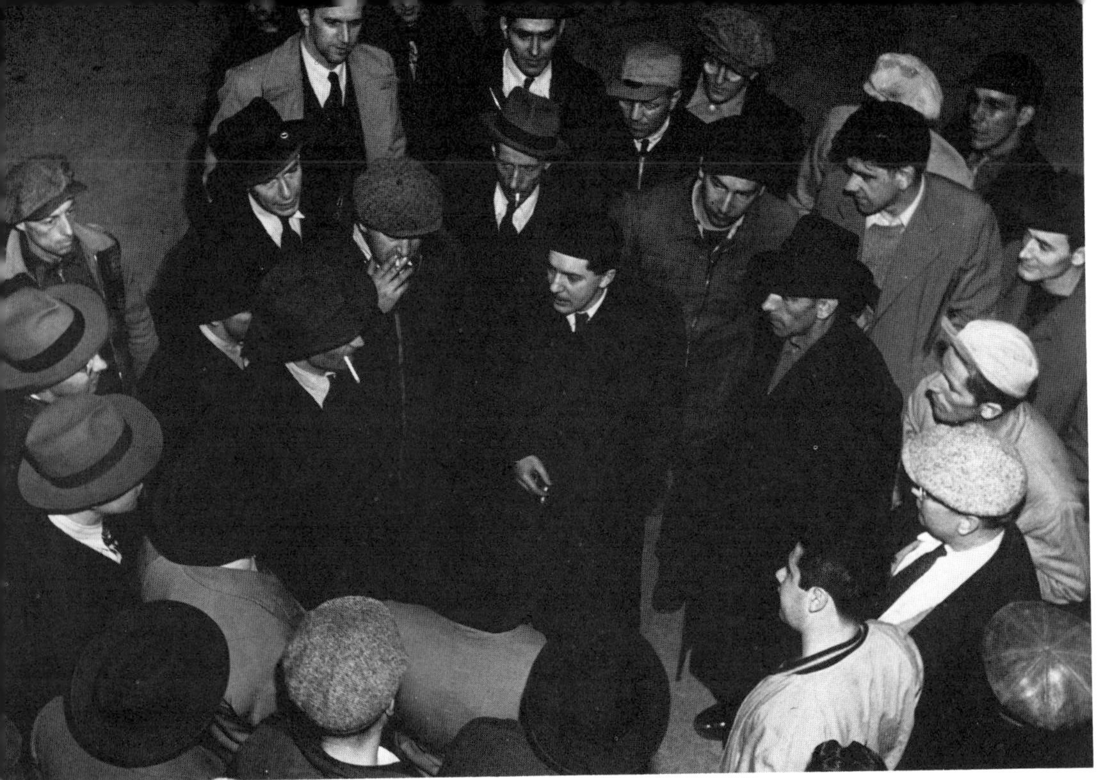

ON STRIKE!

A restless Quebec labour force fought through the decade to improve its situation. Jean Marchand (above centre) led a 135-day strike at Asbestos in 1949. CLC President, Claude Jodoin (below in hat) bolstered Murdochville pickets in 1957.

pension on March 16 for attacking a Boston player with his stick and striking a linesman with his fist the news hit Quebec like the assassination of a cardinal. In the Montreal *Gazette's* composing room, a French-speaking printer broke down and wept. Campbell received dozens of telephoned death threats. In Ottawa, at a Soviet embassy reception, the Russians made a point of commiserating with every Quebecker present.

"Kill Campbell"

When Campbell, in a calm show of defiance, insisted on attending the March 17 game at the Forum, he literally risked his life. The crowd screamed and tried to pelt him with bottles and rotten eggs. When someone threw a tear-gas bomb onto the ice, filling the arena with fumes and emptying the stands, the riot began. At one point there were ten thousand people milling around outside the building, many of them screaming, "Kill Campbell! Kill Campbell!" Then the crowd started smashing the windows of passing streetcars and dragging drivers from their cabs and roughing them up.

When police moved in, the mob started down St. Catherine Street, smashing store windows and looting as they went. Cars were overturned and telephone booths doused with oil and set afire. By the time police dispersed the mob fifteen blocks later, St. Catherine Street was a shambles, seventy people had been arrested, and thirty-seven people, including twelve policemen, had been injured. But Richard's suspension was not the root cause of the crowd's frenzy. In a wider sense, the Anglo-Saxon domination that Campbell represented was the mob's real target.

This domination was becoming more apparent all the time. Quebec was in the middle of an economic boom, and most of the capital which fuelled it was owned by Anglo-Saxons. Technology was moving into Quebec at last, and it carried with it the seeds of Duplessis' downfall. Each new mine, each new factory, each enlarged pay-envelope undermined the ordered, structured society that Duplessis was trying to preserve.

Between 1947 and 1950, new industries in cities like Trois Rivières had created a hundred thousand new jobs and the province found itself in the throes of a full-scale industrial revolution. By 1950 Quebec had the world's highest per capita consumption of electricity, was mining 70 per cent of the world's aluminum, owned more radios per capita than any other Canadian province, and was responsible for fully 31 per cent of Canada's industrial production. A $200-million iron-ore development was getting underway just across the border in Labrador, Anglo-Saxon capital of course, and industrialists were praising Quebec's "stable labour relations," a euphemism for low wages.

incident at Asbestos

The changing industrial climate had already produced some serious conflicts. The Catholic trade unions were gaining in strength and militancy. On the eve of the decade, in 1949, one of the most bitter strikes in Canadian history had exposed the gulf that lay between Duplessis' government and the workers who created the province's wealth. It took place in Asbestos, centre of the mining area that produced 85 per cent of the world's supply of asbestos. The workers' union was asking the Johns-Manville company for more money, higher safety standards and improved working conditions.

Duplessis, whose policies had been consistently anti-labour, declared the strike illegal and sent in the police. For more than four months the strike continued, growing progressively uglier. Provincial police – whom *Le Devoir* charged were being paid a weekly wage by Johns-Manville – harassed strikers and, according to a unanimous resolution of the town council, got drunk "and even rendered themselves guilty of indecent acts in the streets." The strikers retaliated by intimidating men who chose to continue working.

two priests

The tensions erupted when strikers sealed off the town, overturned cars, smashed store windows, beat up non-strikers and took fifteen policemen as prisoners. The following day, a detachment of four hundred provincial police entered the town and quietly restored order. The strike continued for another two months until the company agreed to a ten-cent wage increase (the workers had asked fifteen).

By far the most significant aspect of the strike was that the church had publicly opposed Duplessis. Archbishop Charbonneau of Montreal supported the workers from the pulpit and raised $167,000 for the strikers. "This is a conspiracy to destroy the working class," he told his parishioners, "and it is the church's duty to intervene." The fact that Duplessis later succeeded in persuading the church to exile Charbonneau to Victoria, British Columbia, did not alter the fact that, for the first time, the church and government found themselves on the opposite sides of an issue.

In 1956, two priests from the University of Laval's faculty of social sciences, Fathers Gérard Dion and Louis O'Neill issued a pamphlet condemning the immorality of provincial politics. The 1955 election, they wrote, had been characterized by "vote-buying, abuse of the electoral law, threats of reprisal against those who do not support the 'right party,' false oaths, impersonations, corruption of electoral officers" – all of which, they added, "seem to become normal elements of our social life at election time."

Everyone knew how crooked Quebec elections

René Lévesque

René Lévesque, one of the leaders of Montreal's 1959 CBC strike, upon his release from jail. The staff walked out for the right to voice political views on the French-language CBC network. Later, as a minister in the Liberal government of Jean Lesage, Lévesque became an outspoken proponent for a separate Quebec. After the Liberal defeat in 1966, he formed the *Parti Québecois*, which called for Quebec's final withdrawal from Canadian Confederation.

The citizens' candidate Jean Drapeau (left) received congratulations from Maurice Duplessis on his election as Mayor of Montreal in 1954. Drapeau's promise to rid the city of vice and corruption led to a landslide victory.

were; in the 1955 election, fifty-two people were arrested for electoral fraud in Montreal alone. But the O'Neill-Dion pamphlet marked the first time the situation had been deplored aloud, and by members of the church.

The Asbestos strike had been the first in a series of protests throughout the fifties that reflected the emergence of Quebec as a modern industrial state. For some of the protestors, it was the beginning of notable careers. The union leader in the Asbestos strike, Jean Marchand, would later become one of the leaders of Quebec's Quiet Revolution and go on to a federal cabinet post. A strike of CBC television producers in Montreal was led by a chain-smoking news commentator named René Lévesque, who would become Quebec's Natural Resources Minister under Jean Lesage, and still later a separatist. Covering the Asbestos strike for *Le Devoir* was a young reporter named Gérard Pelletier, who was accompanied by his friend from Montreal, Pierre Elliott Trudeau.

Trudeau was one of the founders in 1950 of *Cité Libre,* an anti-Duplessis political journal whose influence vastly exceeded its circulation. In its pages, Trudeau consistently argued for a "democratic revolution" in Quebec, and against the nationalism and separatism that, by the late fifties, were again engaging the attention of Quebec intellectuals. What Quebec needed, he said, was a return to democratic procedures that would enable the province to develop as a modern industrial power. Quebec nationalism, he felt, could only perpetuate the self-obsessed backwardness of the Duplessis era.

Pierre Trudeau, of course, would later come to argue his case for Confederation on a much larger stage. And some of his colleagues, notably Gérard Pelletier and Jean Marchand, eventually would go to Ottawa with him.

Subsequent events proved them to be prophets of the Quiet Revolution that would sweep Quebec after Duplessis' death. Under the Liberal government of Jean Lesage, the province entered an era of social transformation that once and for all swept Quebec into the twentieth century. Despite all the undercurrents of change that animated Quebec throughout the decade, however, Quebec's transformation could not proceed until the old man who had clung to the past had finished dying in Schefferville.

The music of Quebec reflected an intense devotion to the land. Poet and chansonnier *Gilles Vigneault (right) drew his images from rural Quebec; internationally-acclaimed Pauline Julien was more political.*

CHAPTER NINE

The Business of Culture

Art is not beauty. The purpose of art is to enlarge our emotional experience . . .

Alan Jarvis, Director of National Gallery, 1958

"Canadian culture" and "Canadian identity" – those phrases were bandied about with amazing frequency throughout the fifties, at luncheon speeches, in university common rooms, on CBC commentaries, on panel-show debates and in newspaper editorials. Although no one seemed to know exactly what was meant by these terms, all agreed that they were desirable, that we needed more of both, and that American influences were threatening what little we had.

Canadians had plenty to feel inferior about. All the gentler arts, all those elevated pastimes that make the human condition seem slightly less disreputable, seemed alien to the Canadian experience. Drama, the dance and classical music were scarcely known outside the large metropolitan centres, and whenever they surfaced in places like Saskatoon or Halifax, they were generally regarded with, at the warmest, indifference. Nourishment of the mind and spirit was apparently viewed as a pretty marginal proposition.

Throughout the depression and the war, most Canadians had been concerned mainly with questions of basic survival, and such deficiencies did not matter much. With affluence, however, came dissatisfaction, a desire for the finer things. We had learned to be rich, but we had not learned to enjoy it. We now began to see the importance of having our own artists, our own symphonies, our own folk heroes, our own myths. As this awareness grew, so did the awareness that a distressingly large amount of our culture – the films we saw and the books and magazines we read – were imported from the United States.

In addition, Canadians from coast to coast seemed to share the feeling that they were inferior. Anything Canadian was assumed to be second-rate unless it had received the imprimatur of success abroad. Thus, Jean Gascon's *Théâtre du Nouveau Monde* was scarcely taken seriously, at least in English-speaking Canada, until it conquered Paris in 1955. Some of the country's more durable heroes were performers like Guy Lombardo or Yvonne de Carlo, whose claim to Canadianism was the fact that they had left the country at an early age and made it big down south. One of the proudest moments of the decade, for many Canadians, was that Sunday evening in 1958 when Johnny Wayne and Frank Shuster, who had been amusing Canadians for most of the decade. made their first appearance under the twenty-six-appearance contract they had received from the "Ed Sullivan Show." American television critics considered their Shakespearian skits daringly highbrow, and Sullivan himself told them: "In six months

The Rt. Hon. Vincent Massey

Canada's first native-born governor general, Vincent Massey was also an avid supporter of the arts. In 1949, he was chosen to head the Royal Commission inquiry into the state of culture in Canada. The 1951 Massey Report was regarded by many as the springboard for indigenous talent.

Stars of Stage, Screen and TV

The faces that headline the following six pages make an impressive gallery of stars who became recognized round the world for excellence on stage and screen. It is a varied collection of Canadian talent. Some made it here while others went to England, Europe or the U.S.

Lorne Greene – stage, screen and TV actor, born in Ottawa, best known for his role as "Ben Cartwright" in television's "Bonanza" series.

Jay Silverheels – screen and TV actor, born in Brantford, alias "Tonto" of the 1950's television series, "The Lone Ranger."

William Shatner – screen and TV actor, born in Montreal, best known for his role as "Captain Kirk" on the popular "Star Trek" series.

you'll be the hottest product on American TV." When Wayne and Shuster elected to continue living in Toronto, there were newspaper editorials praising their patriotism.

Education would have been one means of achieving the self-assurance we so sadly lacked; but in the early fifties our schools did not hold much promise for a cultural renaissance. Having graduated only recently from an agrarian economy, Canadians tended to regard education not as a necessary social investment, but as an amenity that could be useful if accomplished cheaply and if not pursued to extremes. As late as 1953, fewer than half the country's ninety thousand teachers had graduated from high school. The teacher shortage was desperate – at least ten thousand more were needed – but salaries were abysmally low. In 1949, when doctors earned an average of $9,000, the average Canadian teacher earned $1,885. Most teachers in Prince Edward Island were paid less than $1,500 a year. Moonlighting had become a way of life for teachers across the country. In Halifax, two teachers doubled as radio announcers in the evening, and a third as a garage mechanic. Ottawa's Catholic School Board used to employ some of its teachers as grounds-keepers during the summer holidays; the board paid them better to mow lawns than it did to mould young minds. In rural Manitoba, a survey revealed that only 13 per cent of the pupils studied in classrooms equipped with electric lights, and that 88 per cent attended schools with outdoor privies.

A 1954 book by Dr. Hilda Neatby, of the University of Saskatchewan, however, caught the imagination of the Canadian public. It went through a second printing and a new edition within the first three months. The book was called *So Little for the Mind* and it advanced the proposition that Canada's educational establishment was dominated by nitwits and intellectual frauds. Dr.

Don Harron – stage and screen actor, playwright and comedian, born in Toronto, alias "Charlie Farquharson" since the 1953 "Spring Thaw."

Norman Campbell – musician, composer, producer, born in Los Angeles, best known for the music of "Anne of Green Gables."

Kate Reid–dramatic actress, best known for brilliant performances at Stratford and in New York roles such as Who's Afraid of Virginia Woolf?

Norman Jewison – movie producer and director, born in Toronto, known for Fiddler on the Roof, Jesus Christ, Superstar, *and other films.*

Neatby's main target was "progressive education," which she described as anti-intellectual, anti-cultural and amoral. She called for an abandonment of the mushy educational philosophy of "life-adjustment" and a return to intellectual discipline. Although many disagreed with Neatby's statements, the book did focus attention on the intellectual climate in our school system.

As early as 1950, it was becoming apparent that our neglect of cultural and intellectual matters was creating a potential threat to the nation's survival. Mordecai Richler's first novel sold two hundred copies in Canada; the world's largest totem-pole collection was located in Berlin, rather than Vancouver; and the chief patrons by far of Canadian cultural and scientific pursuits were the Carnegie and Rockefeller Foundations. American periodicals enjoyed a circulation in Canada more than twice as large as that of Canadian magazines. Our dependence on American cultural artifacts, from textbooks and soap operas to crime comics and symphony broadcasts, was very nearly total. "We must not be blind," remarked Vincent Massey, "to the very present danger of permanent dependence."

Massey was chairman of the Royal Commission on National Development in the Arts, Letters and Sciences, a federal inquiry that lasted for two years and revealed the extent of our cultural impoverishment. Reporting in 1951, the commission recommended increased efforts to preserve the Canadian character of our broadcasting, and scores of other measures designed to lessen Canada's dependence on American cultural influences. One of its most important recommendations was for the creation of a Canada Council that would aid universities and subsidize creative and scientific efforts.

Thanks to the fortuitous demise of two multi-millionaires whose estates yielded the government

Arthur Hiller – television and screen director, born in Edmonton, known for his films The Americanization of Emily *and* The Out-of-Towners.

Christopher Plummer – screen and stage actor, born in Toronto, best known for his roles in The Sound of Music, Waterloo *and others.*

Bruno Gerussi – stage, screen and television actor, born in Vancouver, best known for his work in radio and CBC's "The Beachcombers."

Gratien Gélinas – actor, director and founder of the famous Théâtre du Nouveau Monde, born in St. Tite, a small town near Trois Rivières.

a $50-million tax windfall, the Canada Council was established in 1957. Its beginnings were fairly inauspicious. One Social Credit MP, John Blackmore, warned Parliament that it would subvert religion, patriotism and family life. During its first thirty months, the Council had to decline requests for grants from people who wanted to build an aquarium, design a new Canadian flag and erect a chain of luxurious roadside comfort-stations. A man in California was denied a subsidy to write a song about the Dionne Quintuplets, and one Canadian inventor asked for, but did not receive, a grant to assist him in patenting a revolutionary new brassiere.

The requests that the Council did grant over a period of years had several encouraging effects. Although the works its subsidies made possible were not always masterpieces, the Council did help to create a climate that encouraged intellectual innovation. Of course, the Canada Council recipient idling away in Mexico or the Balearics quickly became a national folk-image.

The effects of the Council were mild, however, compared to the effect of a seemingly unimportant event: Russia's launching in 1957 of the world's first space satellite. The effect in North America was electric and instantaneous. Suddenly the continental power structure discovered that education, which it had so badly neglected for so long, could be a practical proposition. The press carried hundreds of stories contrasting the relentless excellence of Soviet education with the waste, ineptitude and frivolity of the North American product. "Russia," warned University of Toronto President Claude Bissell, "is adding to its intellectual class far faster than Canada." Another Toronto professor, after a visit to Moscow, noted an even more disturbing symptom: Moscow University residences had one bathroom for every two students, while at U. of T. there was only one for each floor.

Barbara Hamilton – comedienne of a thousand faces, born in Toronto, best known for her zany roles in "Spring Thaw" and various revues.

Gisèle MacKenzie–popular pianist, vocalist and violinist, born in Winnipeg, best known for the CBC*'s "Meet Gisèle" on both radio and* TV.

Fletcher Markle – screen and TV director, born in Winnipeg, best known for Jigsaw, Night Into Morning *and his CBC-TV drama.*

Glenn Gould – classical concert and recording pianist, born in Toronto, best known for his performances of the works of Bach and Beethoven.

Most of this concern was well founded and it quickly led to results. Sputnik suddenly made it respectable, indeed mandatory, for hard-headed men to support educational investments. The new climate was reflected in school expenditures, which showed a sharp upturn after 1957.

State intervention, then, was an important factor in warming the country's intellectual climate. Our most notable achievements, however, were still the work of dedicated and frequently frustrated individuals. Many of them were recent arrivals to Canada, people who could not understand why a nation of fifteen million did not have a national ballet company, or a first-class symphony orchestra or a major theatrical festival. They worked in their own communities or, like Celia Franca, Alan Jarvis and Mavor Moore, on a national scale. But all of them had to contend with lack of money, massive indifference, scorn and the acoustics of high-school gymnasiums. Quite a few of these individual efforts were unrewarding, but some were simply magnificent.

Stratford was unquestionably the most successful, and the most inspirational. It started as a crazy idea in the head of an English immigrant named Tom Patterson, who persuaded the city council of Stratford, Ontario, to give him $125 for a trip to New York. He hoped to persuade Sir Laurence Olivier to come to Stratford to mount a Shakespearian festival. He never got to see Olivier; instead, he phoned Tyrone Guthrie, who agreed for a $500 fee to fly from England to investigate the proposition.

Guthrie came, saw Stratford, and decided to take the gamble. He brought in Alec Guinness and stage designer Tanya Moiseiwitsch and set to work. The Stratford Festival held its first season in 1953 in a modified circus tent seating 1,500 people beside the Avon River, and it made Stratford, a conservative farming town, into the world's most

Oscar Peterson – internationally renowned jazz pianist, composer and arranger, born in Montreal; his credits and accolades are legion.

Moe Koffman – jazz composer, musician and arranger, born in Toronto, still known for his hit single of the 50s, "Swinging Shepherd Blues."

Melissa Hayden – prima ballerina with the New York City Ballet, born in Toronto, best known for her role of Clorinda, in The Duel.

Maureen Forrester – contralto with the Berlin and London Opera Companies, born in Montreal, known both for her concerts and recordings.

improbable theatrical centre. From the start it was a community effort; local firms donated $50,000 and outside industry contributed another $100,000. Everyone in town was affected, for the summer performances attracted a thousand carloads of visitors every day. Celebrities like Duke Ellington or *New York Times* drama critic Brooks Atkinson stopped being a novelty. Queen Street North was renamed Guthrie Avenue. One farmer cancelled his subscription to the *Beacon-Herald* because he objected to all the "Shakespeare propaganda."

The Stratford miracle became an inspiration for cultural crusaders across the country. Despite apathy, skepticism and a shortage of funds, one man, Tom Patterson, had mobilized an ordinary town into doing something great. The experience was life-enhancing, and it was fun. Life became more interesting in Stratford, and you could see it in a hundred ways. The local picture-framing shop started selling fewer mirrors and more reproductions of good paintings. One local grocery began stocking exotic things like Greek honey, Mexican fried worms, truffles and canned bird's nest soup. Businessmen noticed that, in the four-year period after the festival began, Stratford attracted twice as many new industries as it did in the previous four years. The message was clear: culture, like education, could be practical.

Stratford was a triumph, and it is no denigration of its achievement to note that it was accomplished largely by imported talent. "We must not try to annex the project and use it for our own private advancement," Tyrone Guthrie wrote Alec Guinness before the festival's first season. "It should be a Canadian scheme carried through by Canadians." The hope he expressed was laudable, but difficult to achieve. As late as the 1958 season, more than half the cast were British-trained and nine of the fourteen backstage personnel were

George London – bass-baritone with New York's Metropolitan Opera, born in Montreal; performances during a too-brief career were SRO.

Jon Vickers – operatic tenor, born in Prince Albert, performed frequently at Stratford, and with every major festival and company in the world.

Teresa Stratas – coloratura soprano with the London Opera Company, born in Toronto, widely acclaimed for performances like Carmen.

Lois Marshall – mezzo-soprano, born in Toronto, made her debut at New York Town Hall, and in London with the Royal Philharmonic.

British. Even the costume-cutting department had to import a British expert. This underlined the fact that we needed training facilities for everyone from actors to museum directors. By the end of the decade we were beginning to get those facilities. The founding of the National Theatre School in Montreal was partially a by-product of Stratford, and so was the increased interest in fine arts courses at universities across the country.

And so it began to happen. Celia Franca, another determined British import, melded together a few private dance schools and a handful of talented dancers into the National Ballet, an organization that was to become one of the world's great dance companies. Vancouver mounted its own performing arts festival in 1958, spending $400,000 to assemble artists and performing troupes from across Canada and around the world. The big names included Glenn Gould, Bruno Walter, Maureen Forrester and Lister Sinclair, who offered a new play called *The World of The Wonderful Dark*. Like its predecessors in Edinburgh and Stratford, Vancouver's festival focussed on the performing arts but sponsored a string of ancillary events as well, including a film festival and jazz concerts.

As the decade progressed, increasing numbers of people became impatient at the lack of cultural amenities and succeeded in doing something about it. Adult education flourished. A million Canadians enrolled in night-school courses in 1958 to brush up on everything from dog-training to philosophy to coal-mining, and some fourteen thousand Canadians were members of film societies. In 1959, Mordecai Richler published *The Apprenticeship of Duddy Kravitz*, and Hugh MacLennan published *The Watch That Ends the Night*. The Canada Council gave $60,000 to the Canadian Opera Company, which sent out two highly professional troupes to present live opera in nine prov-

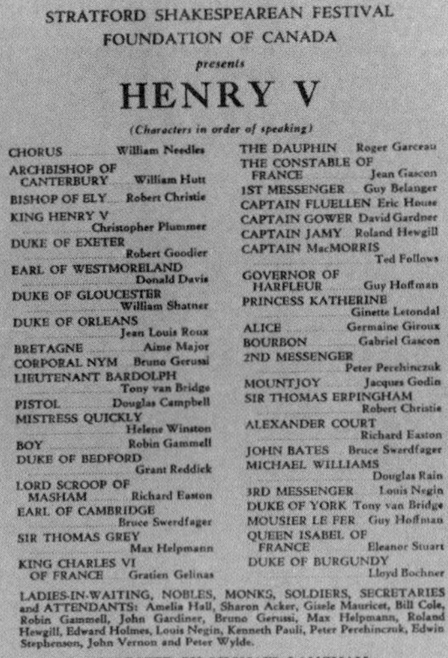

STRATFORD SHAKESPEAREAN FESTIVAL
FOUNDATION OF CANADA

presents

HENRY V

(Characters in order of speaking)

CHORUS ... William Needles
ARCHBISHOP OF CANTERBURY ... William Hutt
BISHOP OF ELY ... Robert Christie
KING HENRY V ... Christopher Plummer
DUKE OF EXETER ... Robert Goodier
EARL OF WESTMORELAND ... Donald Davis
DUKE OF GLOUCESTER ... William Shatner
DUKE OF ORLEANS ... Jean Louis Roux
BRETAGNE ... Aime Major
CORPORAL NYM ... Bruno Gerussi
LIEUTENANT BARDOLPH ... Tony van Bridge
PISTOL ... Douglas Campbell
MISTRESS QUICKLY ... Helene Winston
BOY ... Robin Gammell
DUKE OF BEDFORD ... Grant Reddick
LORD SCROOP OF MASHAM ... Richard Easton
EARL OF CAMBRIDGE ... Bruce Swerdfager
SIR THOMAS GREY ... Max Helpmann
KING CHARLES VI OF FRANCE ... Gratien Gelinas
THE DAUPHIN ... Roger Garceau
THE CONSTABLE OF FRANCE ... Jean Gascon
1ST MESSENGER ... Guy Belanger
CAPTAIN FLUELLEN ... Eric House
CAPTAIN GOWER ... David Gardner
CAPTAIN JAMY ... Roland Hewgill
CAPTAIN MacMORRIS ... Ted Follows
GOVERNOR OF HARFLEUR ... Guy Hoffman
PRINCESS KATHERINE ... Ginette Letondal
ALICE ... Germaine Giroux
BOURBON ... Gabriel Gascon
2ND MESSENGER ... Peter Perehinczuk
MOUNTJOY ... Jacques Godin
SIR THOMAS ERPINGHAM ... Robert Christie
ALEXANDER COURT ... Richard Easton
JOHN BATES ... Bruce Swerdfager
MICHAEL WILLIAMS ... Douglas Rain
3RD MESSENGER ... Louis Negin
DUKE OF YORK ... Tony van Bridge
MOUSIER LE FER ... Guy Hoffman
QUEEN ISABEL OF FRANCE ... Eleanor Stuart
DUKE OF BURGUNDY ... Lloyd Bochner

LADIES-IN-WAITING, NOBLES, MONKS, SOLDIERS, SECRETARIES and ATTENDANTS: Amelia Hall, Sharon Acker, Gisele Mauricet, Bill Cole, Robin Gammell, John Gardiner, Bruno Gerussi, Max Helpmann, Roland Hewgill, Edward Holmes, Louis Negin, Kenneth Pauli, Peter Perehinczuk, Edwin Stephenson, John Vernon and Peter Wylde.

DIRECTED BY MICHAEL LANGHAM
DESIGNED BY TANYA MOISEIWITSCH
MUSIC BY LOUIS APPLEBAUM
Conducted by John Cook

For Canadian actors and stage buffs the birth of the Stratford Festival was the most ambitious undertaking in the cultural history of the nation. This cast for Henry V *reads like a Who's Who of the Canadian stage.*

inces, and a Quebec *chansonnier* named Felix Leclerc earned an estimated $100,000 singing folk songs about his native province.

Calgary's glossy Southern Alberta Jubilee Auditorium opened its doors, boosting that city's attendance at serious cultural events by 35 per cent, and hastening the day when Canadians would grow intolerant of symphony concerts and operas that were presented in hockey rinks. Vancouver's Queen Elizabeth Theatre and Toronto's O'Keefe Centre, which opened in 1960, were forerunners of a nation-wide string of publicly financed centres for the performing arts.

There was only one drawback. All these developments were relentlessly middle-class. The arts remained essentially a monopoly of the educated and the established. Popular culture – the dance bands, the jazz musicians, the comedians, the clowns – was almost exclusively imported from abroad. It would be almost another decade before the realization sank in that "Canadian culture" did not have to be elitist.

Still, there was some progress in this frivolous direction. Most encouraging was the fact that for almost the first time we managed to laugh at ourselves. *Spring Thaw,* the annual satirical revue, flourished through the 1950s. *Clap Hands,* a one-shot revue staged in Toronto in 1958 (and later in London), spoofed such urgent Canadian topics as Marani-Morris, a firm of architects who specialized in dull, slablike office buildings. The most popular theatrical production of the decade sprang, almost by accident, from the campus of McGill University. It was a joyous musical send-up of everything Canadian called *My Fur Lady.* Written, produced, directed and acted by students, it kidded the St. Laurent government, as in this lyric by a chorus of docile Liberal backbenchers:

> *Send a note, send a note, tell us how to vote*
> *Uncle Lou, Uncle Lou, tell us what to do – and Howe!*

Mercifully, it also spoofed the cultural mafiosi that, in the wake of the Massey Report, had emigrated from Britain to bring uplift to the colonials.

The show quickly outgrew its undergraduate origins and went on a coast-to-coast tour. By the spring of 1958, *My Fur Lady* had played 313 performances to 214,000 people across the country and grossed a half-million dollars.

The interesting aspect of all these cultural developments was that very few of them were consciously, distinctively *Canadian.* There was excellence: painters like Jean-Paul Riopelle and Harold Town, singers like Lois Marshall, pianists like Oscar Peterson and Glenn Gould. But their talent transcended national boundaries. They were artists first, and incidentally Canadians. No one wrote a great "Canadian" novel, no one composed a "Canadian" symphony, no painter emerged who reflected his country as much as his or her own individual perceptions.

The cumulative effect of all these individual efforts, however, was encouraging. It may not have been "Canadian" excellence, but it was excellence by Canadians. In that awareness lay the beginnings of self-assurance – the foundations of "Canadian culture" and "Canadian identity," the foundation that had eluded us for so long.

When Art Went Wild

Canadian painting went wild in the fifties as radical artists like Harold Town in Toronto, Roy Kiyooka in Saskatchewan and Alfred Pellan in Montreal rejected traditional landscape painting and experimented with bold new abstract ways of expression. Liberation from conventional forms came first in Quebec with Alfred Pellan, Paul-Emile Borduas and Jean-Paul Riopelle. In 1953, Painters Eleven, a loosely-associated group of abstract expressionists who banded together in Toronto, offered Canadians an alternative to representational art and the heritage of the Group of Seven.

In 1955, during his first year as Director of the National Gallery, Brantford-born Alan Jarvis (centre) spent over $90,000 on modern abstract paintings by Canadian artists. Although his many critics denounced these purchases as a "farce," Jarvis steadfastly proclaimed them to be "the most creative work" being done in Canada. Two of the many artists that Jarvis supported were Alfred Pellan (right), a key figure in the Quebec art revolution, and Harold Town (left), the most flamboyant member of Painters Eleven.

Some Abstract Expressionists

Et Le Soleil Continue, *Alfred Pellan, 1959. Pellan was given the honour of a one-man show at Le Musée d'Art Moderne, Paris, in '55.*

Airy Journey, *Jock Macdonald, 1957. An original member of Painters Eleven.*

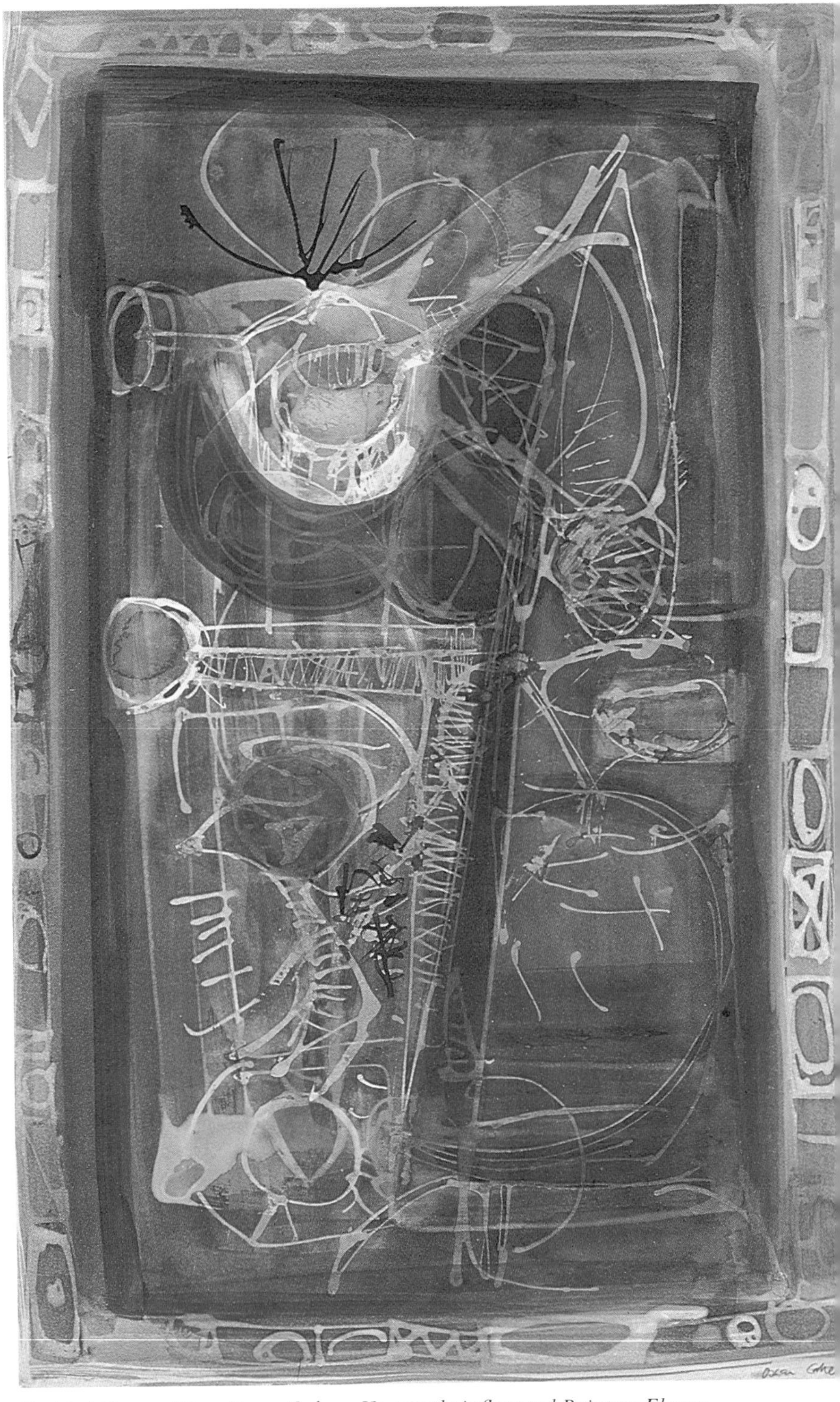

Untitled Composition, Oscar Cahen. He greatly influenced Painters Eleven.

'he Fence, *Harold Town, 1959-60. Town's reputation as a ·ainter began in '52. By '56, he was exhibiting abroad.*

J'Accuse, *William Ronald, 1956. The artist was a student of Jock Macdonald in the early fifties.*

'he Dignitary, *Kenneth Lochhead, 1953. At age 24, Lochhead was appointed Director of the University of Saskatchewan's School of Art.*

TELEPHONE

CHAPTER TEN

Campus Capers

. . . we have plenty of 20th century schools filled with 19th century teachers.

A.R.M. Lower, 1958

He was later to become a successful Vancouver lawyer. In the spring of 1954, however, Clive Nylander decided to run for student council president at the University of British Columbia under the nickname by which he was then known: Baru. He had not a hope of winning, but he and a dozen other law students spent most of their waking hours for weeks on a campaign that blanketed the UBC campus with hand-lettered campaign posters and clever slogans like "The West, a Nest and Baru, Dear." Two days before the election, a fellow law student, who worked nights as a typesetter on the campus newspaper, *The Ubyssey,* nudged the campaign along by resetting the paper's logo to read *The Barubyssey*. By the eve of the election, the "serious" candidates were beginning to worry that Baru might actually get elected. To his own relief, however, Baru finished fourth in a field of four.

The Baru for President campaign pretty accurately summarized the tone of campus life. For large numbers of the 72,729 undergraduates who attended Canadian universities in the mid-fifties, higher education consisted of three or four years of almost unexampled idleness, frivolity and, frequently, dissipation. Serious work and feverish study was going on, no doubt, in the science faculties, professional schools and graduate schools. But although there was feverish cramming at exam time in every faculty, the undergraduates set the tone for Canada's universities, and for most of them, acquiring a degree was a matter of almost sinful ease.

By the end of the decade, rising enrolments and increased competition for university places would begin to turn higher education into an earnest business. But from 1946, when returning war veterans swamped the universities, to 1957, when the Soviet Union launched the world's first space satellite and shocked the United States into an awareness of the deficiencies of the North American educational system, campus life seemed to consist of one long party – a halcyon decade of beer busts, Homecoming Balls, mock kidnappings, drunken thefts from rival schools (usually a cannon or a statue), good-humoured riots, football weekends, fraternity initiations, snake dances, pep rallies, sorority serenades, bonfires, chariot races, pranks, mock elections and fake scandals engineered by college newspapers.

There were few causes, apart from occasional protests about the quality of cafeteria food, that any significant number of students cared about. (The most passionate demonstration anyone at UBC can remember occurred around 1956, when

TOIKE OIKE

TOIKE OIKE TOIKE OIKE OLLUM TE CHOLLUM TE CHAY SCHOOL OF SCIENCE SCHOOL OF SCIENCE HURRAY HURRAY HURRAY

HYDRANT PUP RESIGNS

ELECTION COMMENTS

EDGEWORTH DEBATE FINALS

PROFESSIONAL ASSOCIATIONS

PROFESSIONAL? BAH!

DEAN FINISHES UNETHICAL DISCUSSIONS

The engineering students at U of T concocted an uproarious news and nonsense paper called Toike Oike. *The paper's irreverent treatment of "skule" life raised eyebrows in faculty lounges, but created howls of laughter in the student dorms.*

Opposite page: *Autumn months in most university towns during the fifties were coloured by student hi-jinks and general craziness.*

students picketed the Vancouver *Sun* to protest cancellation of the comic strip, *Pogo*.) There were few sexual outlets, either. The cumulative effect of all that hot young frustration, all those frantic but unconsummated grapplings in the front and back seats of all those Chevys and Buicks and Pontiacs and Model A's, must have contributed to the level of ambient energy that was available for rechannelling into various idle pursuits.

Despite their popularity with students, jeans were banned from high schools and university campuses in the fifties.

co-educational hanky-panky

Nor was there much in the way of organized, off-campus diversion. In most Canadian cities, undergraduates experienced the same deprivations as their elders during the early part of the decade: there were few good cheap restaurants, few cocktail bars, few places to dance, few concerts or other cultural events. There were few opportunities, in other words, for undergraduates to fan out and become members of the surrounding community. Instead, universities tended to be undergraduate ghettoes that had few contacts with the cities that harboured them. At Mount Allison University, in Sackville, New Brunswick, nearly 90 per cent of the student body lived on campus in residences that were rigidly policed by sharp-eyed faculty members, trained to detect the least sign of co-educational hanky-panky. "They used to tell us it was an 'experiment in living,'" recalls one graduate. "But in fact it was more like prison."

Even when undergraduates did penetrate downtown, they did not do so simply as people. Instead, they tended to congregate at various coffee shops and pubs that were patronized almost exclusively by other students. At the University of Toronto, it was the King Cole Room at the Park Plaza Hotel. At UBC, where students had to drive eight miles to the nearest legal glass of beer, it was the basement tavern of the Hotel Georgia.

Finally, there wasn't much competition. This

Masterminds of Medicine

Throughout the fifties, doctors in Canadian labs made medical headlines with research into stress, Vitamin E and neurology. Discoveries outside the country gave us the revolutionary birth control pill, the Salk polio vaccine and antihistamines.

Dr. Hans Selye of the University of Montreal was the first to detail and measure the effects of stress on the body.

World renowned surgeon, philosopher and bestselling author Dr. Wilder Penfield charted the intricate human brain.

Biochemist Dr. Evan Shute of London, Ontario, aroused the curiosities of medics with controversial work in Vitamin E.

was the last decade in which Canadian universities could be described as elitist. Only a small proportion of the country's high-school graduates went on to university. And once they graduated they could be reasonably assured of getting a job. Corporate recruiters from such firms as Procter & Gamble and IBM actually courted Bachelor of Arts graduates. For graduates of such specialized faculties as engineering and business administration, the problem was often to choose from among offers from several competing corporations.

If the certainty of future employment lent a certain carelessness to campus life, so did the mere fact of being there. Going to university was still something special, like going to Europe: a privilege and a pleasure reserved mainly for the upper middle class. The University of Toronto still asked on its admission forms if the applicant's parents were U OF T graduates; several other universities did the same.

sweet autumn of idleness

Academic standards were often high and flunking out, especially in freshman year, was still a distinct possibility. "Look at the man on your right," one U OF T professor told his freshman class in 1958, "and now take a good look at the man on your left. One of you isn't going to be here by the end of the year." In most universities, however, marking schemes were structured so that class work counted for very little, and Christmas and final exams counted for almost everything. This stress on examinations imposed a cyclical pattern on undergraduate life: a sweet autumn of idleness, interrupted by a brief but frantic burst of cramming just before Christmas; then a further few months of leisurely non-achievement stretching from January to mid-March, followed by a further bout of even more intense cramming that lasted until the end of exams early in May.

Father's old felt hat could easily be converted into the genuine "Jughead" beanie, an essential initiation prop.

Frat Follies

Eager new arrivals on campus recited fairytales, kidnapped upperclassmen and scrubbed sidewalks, competing for the coveted frat invitation that made them campus celebrities.

A 1956 chorus line of frat hopefuls at Queen's rolled up their pant legs and lured one lone co-ed for their romp through Kingston's autumn streets.

Cheerleaders practised long hours and had to attend every game. It was hard work but they were campus stars and they dated the football players.

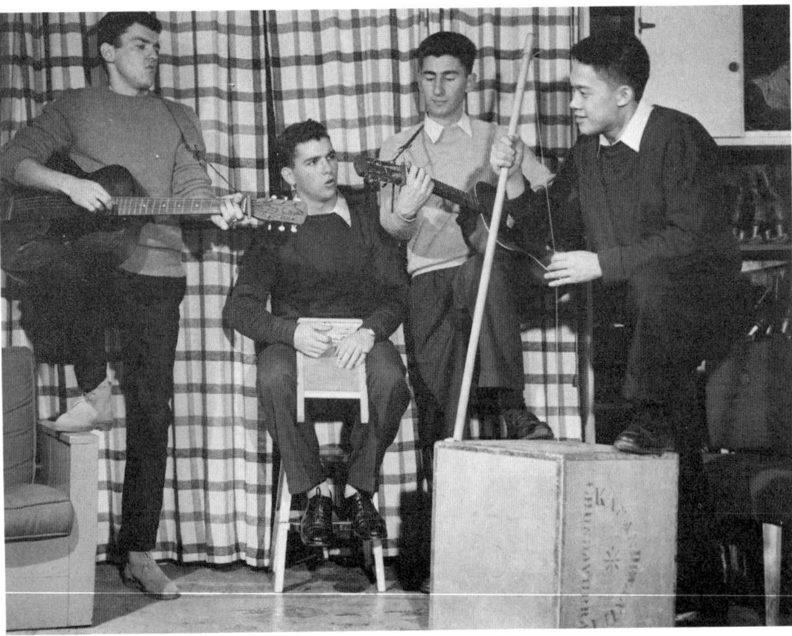

"Skiffle groups" were popular during the fifties, and anyone who could get together a washboard, a broom stick and a guitar was in business.

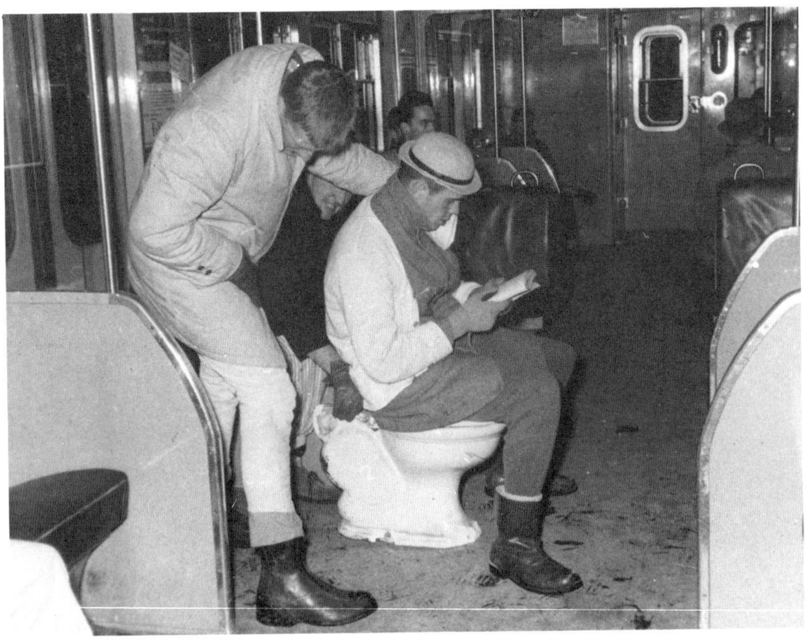

This 1959 Toilet Bowl was sponsored by the University of Toronto chapter of Sigma Nu. Early morning riders on the subway were a captive audience.

It was not a hard life. One of the most onerous aspects, in fact, was enduring the rituals that were as common as falling leaves every autumn on almost every Canadian campus. At Victoria College in the University of Toronto, freshmen were forced to don pyjamas, board the newly-opened subway in pairs and then, before the bemused gaze of late-evening commuters, declaim the love scene from *Romeo and Juliet* while other freshmen, also clad in pyjamas, strolled around the car, selling "tickets" made out of rolls of toilet paper.

"rushing"

At UBC every member of the freshman class was expected to wear purple-and-gold beanies for his or her first week on campus. Female students were officially welcomed with teas and orientation lectures by a sort of anyone-can-join sorority called Phrateres ("Famous for Friendliness.") Male students at UBC got a raunchier welcome: the Frosh Smoker, complete with *legal* beer, inspirational pep-talks by athletic upperclassmen, and a performance by a weary stripper imported from Hastings Street.

Freshmen initiation rites were essentially voluntary. You didn't *have* to wear silly beanies, get chained to lamp-posts, carry the books of upperclassmen or participate in sack-races on the university mall unless you wanted to. But for undergraduates who chose to "rush" – that is, submit themselves to the gruelling, weeks-long process of mutual selection involved in joining a fraternity or sorority – the rites of membership were an earnest, sometimes heart-breaking business. At nearly every large university in the country – the Universities of British Columbia, Alberta, Saskatchewan, Manitoba, and Toronto, and McGill and Dalhousie all tolerated the procedure – "rushing" in the spring and fall obsessed from ten to twenty per cent of the undergraduate population.

Ryerson "freshie" in a beanie drew jeers and smiles from upperclassmen.

Author, Author

The fifties witnessed the emergence and development of several writers who were to become powerful figures in Canadian literature–novelists such as Mordecai Richler, Hugh MacLennan, Robertson Davies, Brian Moore, Adele Wiseman and Ernest Buckler; poets like Irving Layton, Miriam Waddington, Eli Mandel, Jay Macpherson, Leonard Cohen and Alden Nowlan.

Gabrielle Roy recounted childhood experience in rural Manitoba.

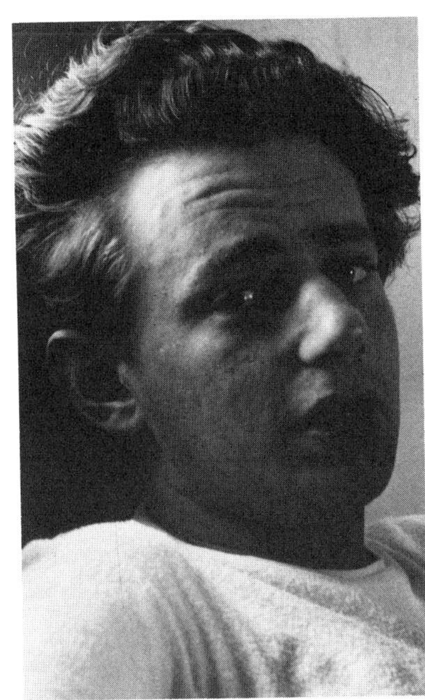

With bitter-sweet humour, Mordecai Richler portrayed Montreal Jews.

Farley Mowat poignantly showed the destruction of the Eskimo life.

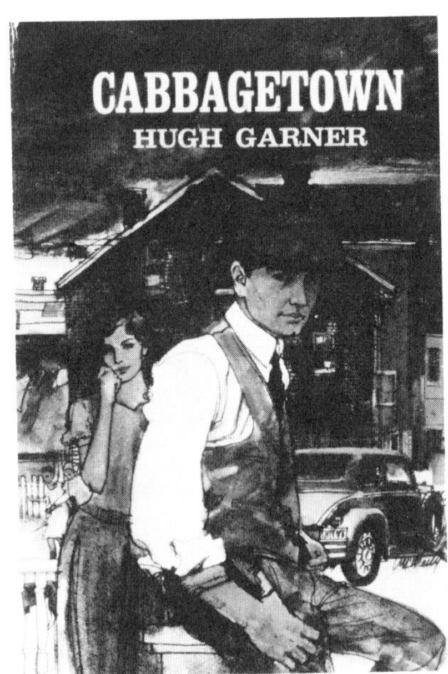

Hugh Garner's chronicle of thirties slum life sold 45,000 copies in '50.

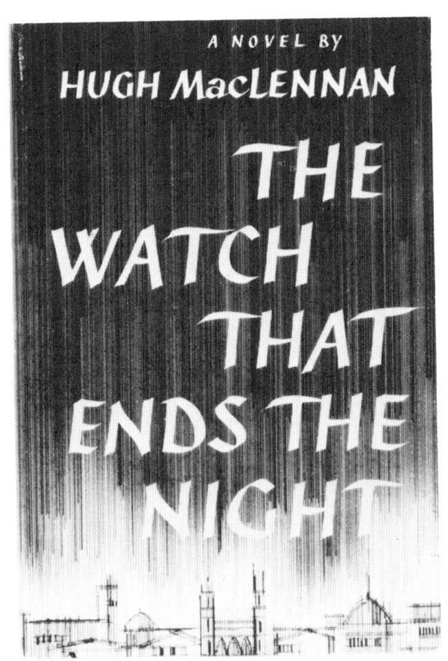

Hugh MacLennan's powerful novel of moral crisis was his fifth, in '59.

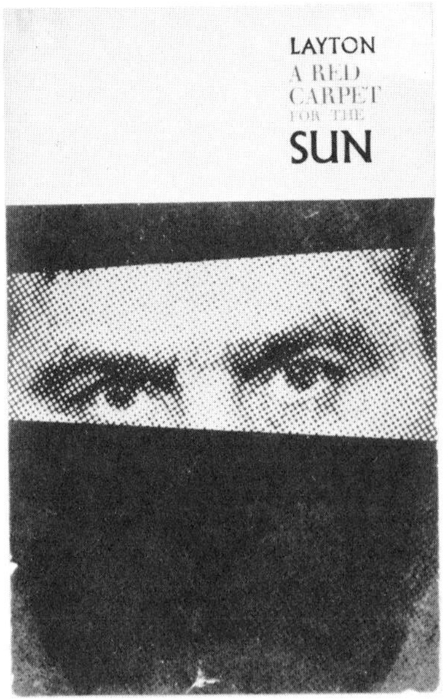

A prolific Irving Layton produced ten volumes of poetry in the fifties.

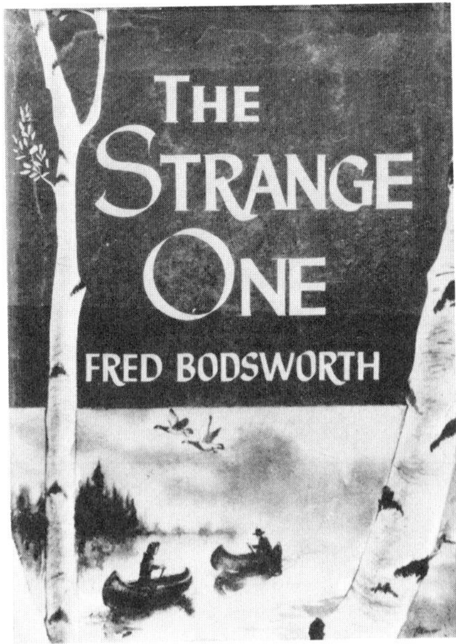

Fred Bodsworth's Cree love story was published in the U.S. in '59.

Rushing consisted of a series of parties or social functions at the frat house (few sororities had houses) where prospective members and their prospective brothers or sisters eyed each other warily, each trying to present as smooth and as pleasing an image as possible. After each party, the members got together for "ding sessions," meetings that were usually either petty or vicious in tone, at which the attributes of each guest were discussed. The most attractive candidates were immediately issued "bids" – engraved invitations inviting them to join; others were asked to still other functions for further assessment. An unfortunate few were not invited back at all. This could occur for a variety of reasons. Some member, for reasons he did not have to explain to his brothers, may have "dinged" (or blackballed) the rushee. The rushee may have exhibited an unacceptable degree of social ineptitude such as wearing sloppy clothes when grey flannels, Harris-tweed sports jackets and white button-down shirts for men and skirts and cashmeres for women were expected. Or he may have gotten *too* drunk; or he may have been Jewish, or at least *looked* Jewish. Accepting a member of other than full Aryan stock was not allowed in most fraternities and sororities in the 1950s, and was expressly forbidden in the constitutions of some.

hugs, handshakes and Hosannahs

Finally came Pledge Day, that long-awaited moment when the rushees – or at any rate those who had received more than one bid – made their fateful choice. For the male pledges it meant welcoming handshakes, hearty back-slaps and a huge party given by their new brothers. For the women, the occasion generated as much emotion as a major beauty pageant. At UBC, the pledges would signal their choice by striding into the cafeteria, where each sorority maintained its own table, and marching to the table of her choice. Hosannahs! The new sister would be greeted by hugs, screams, songs and tears of honest joy. Those who had received bids from only the lowest-ranking sorority, or no bid at all, concealed their humiliation by hiding out for a week or two.

night boat to Powell River

For the male pledges, the serious frivolity now began. Pledgeship, in theory, was a probationary period, although few pledges failed to be initiated a few weeks later as full-fledged brothers. In the meantime, the idea was for pledges and members to play as many pranks on each other as possible. Kidnappings were popular. At UBC, a 1954 pledge class succeeded in kidnapping one of their senior brothers from his bed and depositing him, bound, gagged, and minus his pyjama pants, aboard a reserved stateroom on the night boat to Powell River. Senior brothers retaliated to such provocations by ordering pledges to shine shoes and scrub downtown streets with toothbrushes, or by chaining pledges to lamp posts.

At the end of the probationary period came Initiation Night, which usually lasted an entire weekend. More pranks. There were occasional newspaper reports of brutality at fraternity initiations, but such instances were rare. Instead, the idea was to frighten the initiate as much as possible, without causing actual damage.

Finally the pranks were over, and the pledges were formally initiated. This usually involved a certain amount of mumbo-jumbo in Latin or Greek – and the final unveiling of the society's sacred secrets: the secret handshake, the secret password, the secret recognition signal (such as passing a finger across an eyebrow) by which brothers anywhere in the world might identify themselves to each other, while outsiders remained unaware of the connection.

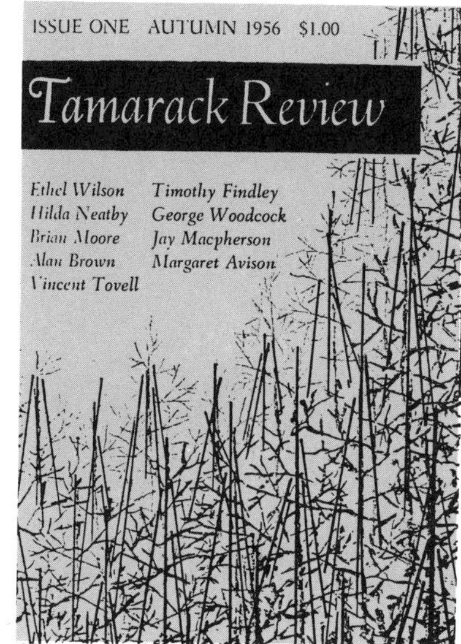

*The decade saw the birth of six new literary magazines–*The Tamarack Review, Canadian Literature, The Waterloo Review, Delta, Prism *and* Alphabet*–which featured both new and established literary talent.*

Cavalcade of Sports

Canadian athletes won an impressive array of medals and titles and set a number of records during the fifties, Curling, boxing, skiing, running, golfing and weightlifting–each contributed moments of excellence.

Skier Lucille Wheeler from St. Jovite, Quebec, won first prize in both giant slalom and the downhill event at the 1958 world championships.

Saskatchewan skip, Ernie Richardson, led Canada to Quebec Brier victory.

Despite a withered leg and sprained ankle, Vancouver's Doug Hepburn won the '53 World Weightlifting Championship in Stockholm. Total lift: 1,030 lbs.

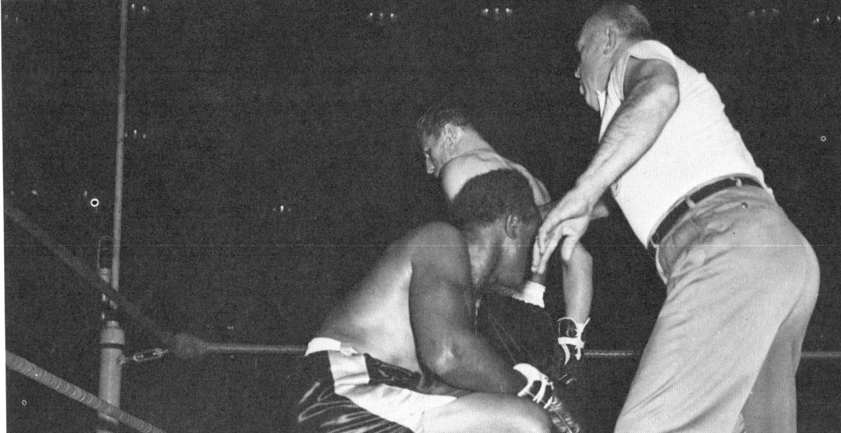

Yvon Durelle floored Archie Moore four times before losing this bout in '58.

Johnny Longden rode 6,000th winner.

Al Balding won 3 tournaments in '57.

Sprinter Harry Jerome established world record of 10 seconds for 100-metre in '59.

Skier Anne Heggtveit captured the gold medal in slalom at '60 Winter Olympics.

First skier ever to make a grand slam of four major events, Ernie McCulloch was elected to U.S. Hall of Fame in '69.

Sam Etcheverry was star quarterback for the Alouettes in '54 Grey Cup game with Eskimos.

'51 Ontario amateur was first golf win for Marlene Stewart.

Campus pranks were by no means limited to fraternity members. Each faculty developed its own style. Law students leaned towards an early variant of guerilla theatre, as when, at McGill, they enrolled a mythical student called Henri d'Ung, signed his attendance sheets at lectures and wrote his exams. D'Ung passed first-year law quite handily. At UBC in 1956, a group of law students calling themselves The Black Hand staged an elaborate *coup d'état* of the students council. The plan was to lure the councillors to a meeting, lock them up, then race across campus to the Armoury, where several thousand students had assembled for the annual general meeting, and announce the takeover. The plan failed, however, because someone forgot the padlock.

Hilda Neatby

Hilda Neatby's explosive book, *So Little for the Mind,* focussed the public's attention on education in 1953 with its savage criticism of progressive education which, she charged, neglected tradition and intellectual discipline in favour of the interests of the student. The publication of the book caused a storm of controversy, as parents and educators rushed to discredit or defend the claims made by the author. A professor of history at the University of Saskatchewan, Dr. Neatby was the one woman member of the Massey Commission.

Lady Godiva Band

On every university campus, it was probably the engineering students who raised more hell than anybody. At almost every faculty in the country, there was a common chant:

We are, we are, we are, we are, we are the engineers,
We can, we can, we can, we can demolish forty beers.
Drink rum, drink rum, you son of a gun, and come along with us,
For we don't give a damn for any old man who don't give a damn for us.

Engineers gloried in their technological expertise, which resulted in countless Volkswagens being taken apart, then reassembled inside somebody's room. At University of Toronto the engineer's showpiece was the Lady Godiva Band, a disreputable musical ensemble that accompanied Lady Godiva, a co-ed clad in flesh-coloured body stocking, on a parade around campus. Rival faculties tried to take their instruments away from them, which usually led to a few bloody noses. At UBC, agriculture students staged an annual chariot race, with home-made carts drawn by students stripped to the waist. Engineers pelted the participants with eggs and rotten fruit. The charioteers replied by pelting the engineers with a fragrant cart-load of sweepings from the Aggie barns.

a time for fun and games

The annual Cake Fight at Trinity College in the University of Toronto was even messier. Freshmen co-eds at neighbouring St. Hilda's college baked a huge cake. First-year Trinity men, surrounding the cake in a phalanx, had to battle their way inside the Trinity quadrangle, while upperclassmen perched on a nearby tower pelted them with anything unspeakable they could find – usually offal and chicken entrails purchased the night before at abattoirs.

Occasionally, these joyous battles got out of hand and spilled over into the surrounding community, and into the headlines. In 1954, a snake dance of Queens University students through the streets of Kingston led to 300 students storming the police station; there were two arrests. In Montreal, McGill students staged a protest march to the Hotel de Ville to protest an impending increase in streetcar fares. The march began with about 300 students in mid-afternoon. By the time it reached its destination, high-school students and assorted toughs from east-end Montreal had joined its ranks, swelling it to an ugly mob of more than a thousand. Someone threw a rock through a tram window – and suddenly it was open season on public transport vehicles. "I can remember going along Sherbrooke Street about 7 P.M. that night," recalls one of the ringleaders, "and there must have been fifteen or twenty buses in total disarray, their tires slashed, their windows smashed. Down on St. Catharine's Street there was a line-up of forty or fifty streetcars – you only have to put one out of commission and they're all out. One estimate of the total damage was a million dollars."

At UBC, two *Ubyssey* columnists wrote a column taunting the engineers, who responded by kidnapping the columnists, kidnapping the Mardi Gras Queen and breaking up a basketball game, with fist-fights breaking out all over the floor, in an attempt to kidnap her escort.

By the late fifties, however, campus capers were beginning to seem a little, well, juvenile. The world moved very close to war during the 1957 Suez crisis, close enough to prompt some students to wonder whether they would be enlisting the way their fathers had eighteen years before. At about the same time, the Hungarian rebellion against Soviet rule sent genuine shock waves through academia, especially after refugees of that tragic uprising enrolled in Canadian universities. These students had fought Russian tanks with paving stones and Molotov cocktails; their intensity and their passionate attachment to freedom provided a strange and disturbing contrast to prevailing undergraduate mores.

It seemed to peter out with the panty raids – forced, imitative non-events that interested few students and amused only the participants and their elders. When the Soviet Union launched the world's first space satellite in 1957, challenging the technological superiority of the West for the first time, the tone changed completely. The missile gap was narrowing, the baby boom generation was coming, education was becoming a major public priority and the time for fun and games was over.

"...happily I can report a remarkable change of attitude...Phelps not only wants to continue school, but can hardly wait to get to UBC..."

CANADIAN NATIONAL EXHIBITION

Acknowledgements

The 1950s are too recent, and too arbitrarily defined, for a large body of hardcover material to have accumulated about the period. The books that I consulted, accordingly, were useful in verifying personal impressions and in assigning the proper weight to various events. For the feel of the period, however, I had to look elsewhere: to the periodicals (by which Canada was notably well-served in the 1950s), to the better newspapers, to the mail-order catalogues, and to my own remembrances.

I was quite fortunate in being able to draw on the personal recollections of my elders and contemporaries. This is how I found out what it was like in the early days of Canadian television, for example, and what it was like to live in Uranium City in 1958.

For permission to quote from copyright material, acknowledgement is made to the following: Chappell Co., Inc., New York, for "Sh-boom" on page 40; John Luccearotto for "Radisson" on page 55; Alden Nowlan for "Saturday Night" on page 37; and Gordon Sinclair for "Next Week's Highlights on TV" on page 55.

Alexander Ross

The Author

Alexander Ross is a writer and editor who has specialized in business and economics. Currently editor of *Toronto Life* magazine, he has been a columnist for the Toronto *Star* and *The Financial Post,* managing editor of *Maclean's* magazine, a story editor on CBC-TV's *This Hour Has Seven Days* and an editorial writer for the Vancouver *Sun*. He won a National Newspaper Award in 1964 for a newspaper series on Quebec's Quiet Revolution. He is the author of *The Toronto Guidebook* and *The Risk Takers,* a book about Canadian entrepreneurs.

Index

The page numbers in italics refer to illustrations and captions.

Picture Credits

We would like to acknowledge the help and cooperation of the directors and staff of the various public institutions and the private firms and individuals who made available paintings, posters, mementoes, collections and albums as well as photographs and gave us permission to reproduce them. Every effort has been made to identify and credit appropriately the sources of all illustrations used in this book. Any further information will be appreciated and acknowledged in subsequent editions.

The illustrations are listed in the order of their appearance on the page, left to right, top to bottom. Principal sources are credited under these abbreviations:

BCPA British Columbia Provincial Archives
CBC Canadian Broadcasting Corporation
CW Photo Canada Wide
DND Department of National Defence
MS Miller Services
PAC Public Archives of Canada
PC Private Collection

/1 Bank of Canada /2 St. Lawrence Seaway Authority /4 Carling O'Keefe Breweries of Canada Limited /6 MS; MS /7 Gulf Oil Canada /8 Courtesy CP Air /9 Hospital for Sick Children /10 CW /11 PC /12 BCPA; Gilbert A. Milne /13 CW; CW; 48th Highlanders of Canada /14 Globe and Mail, Toronto /15 CW /16 Ken Bell /17 All Norris, The Vancouver Sun /18 Newton, Ottawa; Ontario Ministry of Industry and Tourism /19 CW; Horst Ehricht /20 Wide World Photos /21 CW /22 Franklin Arbuckle, Maclean-Hunter; George Weston Limited; Gooderham & Worts Limited; all others PC /23 Brooke Bond Foods Limited; PC; PC; PC; PC; Carling O'Keefe Breweries of Canada Limited; PC; PC /24 Loblaws Limited; Steinberg's Limited /25 Maclean-Hunter /26 Maclean-Hunter /27 Canada Pictures Limited; Henri Rossier /28 Toronto Telegram /29 Ken Bell /30 Maclean-Hunter; Ken Bell /31 British Leyland Motors Canada Limited /32 Labatt Breweries of Canada Limited /33 Monty Fresco, Camera Press London; Stauffer Systems; Capital Press; Horst Ehricht /34 Ford Motor Company of Canada Ltd., Oakville, Ontario; Ford Motor Company of Canada Ltd., Oakville, Ontario; Ford Motor Company of Canada Ltd., Oakville, Ontario; General Motors of Canada, Ltd.; General Motors of Canada Ltd.; General Motors of Canada, Ltd. /35 Ford Motor Company of Canada Ltd., Oakville, Ontario; Ford Motor Company of Canada Ltd., Oakville, Ontario; Studebaker Corporation; Russell Company; Studebaker Corporation /36 Illustration by David Shaw /37 BMI Canada /38 Ken Bell /39 RCA Victor /40 Excellorec Music Company /41 Ken Bell; John Sebert /42 All from Susan Kiil /43 PAC C 35680 /44 Toronto Telegram; CW /45 United Artists; Clyde Gilmour /46 MCA Records Inc.; © Quality Records Limited 1960; Capital Records; others Brendon J. Lyttle Record Research Services, Toronto /47 Brendon J. Lyttle Record Research Services, Toronto; Record cover artwork reproduced by permission of CBS Records Canada Ltd.; Permission granted by Roulette Records, Inc., 17 West 60th St., New York, N.Y. /48 CBC, Wayne & Shuster /49 CBC, Wayne & Shuster /50 Marshall McLuhan /51 CBC, Lorne Greene /52 CBC, Percy Saltzman; CBC, Foster Hewitt; CBC, Marg Osborne, Charlie Chamberlain; CBC, Tommy Hunter; CBC, Lloyd Robertson, Gordon Sinclair, Toby Robins, Pierre Berton, Joyce Davidson; CBC, Mike Malone, Jerry Austin /53 CBC, Ed McCurdy; CBC, Deanne Taylor, Frank Peddie; CBC, Jack Kane; CBC, Joyce Davidson, Percy Saltzman; CBC, John Luccarotti; CBC; CBC, C. Linder; CBC, Juliette, Billy O'Connor; CBC, Wally Koster, Joyce Hahn /54 CBC, Estate of Peter Whittall; Ken Bell; CBC, Marion Clark; CBC, Robert Goulet, Joyce Sullivan; CBC, Joan Fairfax, Denny Vaughan; CBC, Minerva Urscal, Eric Clavering; CBC; CBC, Barry Morse /55 Gordon Sinclair /56 Roger Lemelin /57 CBC, John Drainie; CBC, Max Ferguson; CW; CBC, Elwood Glover; CBC, Andrew Allan; CBC, Earl Cameron; CBC, James Minifie; CBC, estate of Byng Whittaker; CBC, Lister Sinclair /58 CW /59 PAC Progressive Conservative Party Papers /60 Peter C. Newman /61 General Motors of Canada, Ltd. /62 Ontario Hydro /63 All from Bank of Nova Scotia /64 Bank of Canada /65 Legg Brothers /66-67 Illustrations by Sheila Olsen /68 Carling O'Keefe Breweries of Canada Limited; Confederation Life Insurance Company; James Richardson & Sons, Limited; Hawker Siddeley Canada Ltd.; Polysar; Massey-Ferguson Limited; London Life Insurance Company; Domtar Limited; Bank of Nova Scotia; Canadian National Railways; GWG Limited; Toronto Dominion Bank; Uniroyal Limited; Domtar Limited; Domtar Limited; Kenneth Lochhead; Weston's Limited /69 Bell Canada /70 Herb Nott; Maclean-Hunter; Maclean-Hunter; Maclean-Hunter, Hillyard; Glenbow-Alberta Institute; McCullagh Studio, Toronto /71 Ruggles Photographic House /72 Globe and Mail, Toronto; Public Archives of Ontario; Caterpillar Tractor Company /73 Vancouver Public Library; CW; Bob McCormick, Belleville; CW /74 Imperial Oil Limited /75 Maclean-Hunter; Maclean-Hunter /76 Ma Murray /77 Rex Woods; Franklin Arbuckle; P. Whalley; W. Winter; Rex Woods; Ed McNally /79 Oscar Cahen; W. Winter; James Hill; John Little; Rex Woods; Franklin Arbuckle /80 DND /81 DND /82 PC /83 Pierre Berton; DND; DND /84 Canadair /85 Canadair /86 National Museum of Science and Technology, Aviation and Space Division /87 All Canadian Forces Photos /88 CBC, Sandra O'Neil /89 DND /90-91 PC /92 La Presse, Montreal /93 National Library /94 CW /95 Legg Brothers /96 CW /97 CW; Roy Mitchell Photography, Alexandra Studio Archives /98 CW; CW /99 CW /100 CW; Record Cover Artwork reproduced by permission of CBS Records Canada Ltd. /101 Nott and Merrill, Toronto /102 CBC, Lorne Greene; Warner Brothers; William Shatner /103 Legg Brothers, Don Harron; Herb Nott; Herb Nott; CW /104 Robert J. Smith; Werner Wolff; Stratford Festival Canada, Bruno Gerussi; Maclean-Hunter /105 CW; CBC, Giselle Mackenzie; CW; Herb Nott /106 Oscar Peterson; CBC, Moe Koffman; Melissa Hayden; Maureen Forrester /107 CW; Montreal Star, CW; CBC, Teresa Stratas /108 Mirror Press Limited, Stratford /109 Alfred Pellan; Alan Jarvis; PAC /110 Alfred Pellan; Oscar Cahen; Jock Macdonald /111 Harold Town; William Ronald; Kenneth Lochhead /112 Jack Marshall /113 Engineering Society, U of T /114 London Express News /115 Basil Zarov; Ken Bell; Kellogg Salada Canada Ltd. /116 Montreal Star, CW; PC; James Rogers; Montreal Star, CW; CW /117 John de Visser /118 Photo: Annette Zarov; Kryn-Taconis, Magnum Photos; McClelland & Stewart; McGraw-Hill Ryerson Limited; Macmillan Company of Canada Limited; McClelland & Stewart Limited; Dodd, Mead and Company, Inc. /119 Tamarack Review /120 CW; CW; CW; CW; Legg Brothers; Maclean-Hunter /121 Bill Cunningham, The Province; CW; Montreal Star, CW; CW; CW /122 Hilda Neatby /123 Norris, The Vancouver Sun

1955

Angus L. Macdonald Bridge completed between Halifax and Dartmouth, Nova Scotia.

Canadian troops withdraw from Korea.

Marilyn Bell becomes youngest person to swim English Channel.

Canada's Sports Hall of Fame founded.

Riots erupt at Montreal Forum after "Rocket" Richard's suspension.

Lionel Shapiro wins Governor General's Award for novel, *The Sixth of June.*

Canso Causeway is completed between Cape Breton Island and mainland Nova Scotia.

Canadian Labour Congress formed with Claude Jodoin as President.

Landslide at Nicolet, Quebec, causes $5 million damage.

1956

Tamarack Review founded.

The Tamarack Review

A NEW QUARTERLY OF LITERATURE AND THE ARTS

Issue One contains

STORIES BY *Brian Moore* AND *Timothy Findley*, RECOLLECTIONS OF PORTUGAL BY *Ethel Wilson*, A NEW CYCLE OF POEMS BY *Jay Macpherson*, ARTICLES BY *Hilda Neatby*, *Alan Brown*, AND *Vincent Tovell*, REVIEWS BY *George Woodcock*, *Margaret Avison*, *Dennis Wrong*, AND *Kenneth MacLean*, AND DRAWINGS BY *Aba Bayefsky*.

$1.00 a copy $3.50 a year

39 CHARLES ST. W., TORONTO 5

John Jaramey becomes first man to swim Lake Ontario.

Gulf Oil acquires control of British American Oil.

Canadian Football League established.

Gerry Ouellette wins Olympic gold medal at Melbourne for shooting.

UBC Four wins Olympic gold medal in rowing.

Adele Wiseman wins Governor General's Award for novel, *The Sacrifice.*

Robert Stanfield becomes premier of N.S.

John G. Diefenbaker captures Tory leadership.

First trans-Atlantic telephone cable completed between Newfoundland and Scotland.

Liberals force closure of Trans-Canada Pipeline debate.

1957

Lester Pearson receives Nobel Peace Prize for resolution of Suez Crisis.

Fowler Commission Report on Broadcasting published.

Diplomat Herbert Norman commits suicide in Cairo, Egypt.

Ellen Fairclough becomes Secretary of State, first woman appointed to Cabinet post.

Walter Gordon's Commission Report on Canada's Economic Prospects published.

Soviet Union launches Sputnik I and II.

John Diefenbaker leads Tories to minority victory.

Immigration to Canada peaks at 282,000.